Partnership with Parents in Reading

447

UKRA Teaching of Reading Monographs

Advisory editor 1985–
Colin Harrison, Lecturer in Education
School of Education, Nottingham University

Partnership with Parents in Reading
Wendy Bloom

Advisory editor 1984–5
Asher Cashdan, Head of Department of Communication Studies,
Sheffield City Polytechnic

The Emergence of Literacy
Nigel Hall

Teaching Information Skills through Project Work
David Wray

Reading: Tests and Assessment Techniques
Second edition
Peter D. Pumfrey

Children's Writing in the Primary School
Roger Beard

Advisory editors 1977–83
Asher Cashdan
Alastair Hendry, Principal Lecturer in Primary Education,
Craigie College of Education

Listening to Children Reading
Helen Arnold

The Thoughtful Reader in the Primary School
Elizabeth Wilson

Advisory editor 1971–7
John E. Merritt, Professor of Education Studies,
The Open University, Milton Keynes

Print and Prejudice
Sara Goodman Zimet (with an additional chapter by Mary Hoffman)

Partnership with Parents in Reading

Wendy Bloom

Hodder and Stoughton
In association with the United Kingdom Reading Association

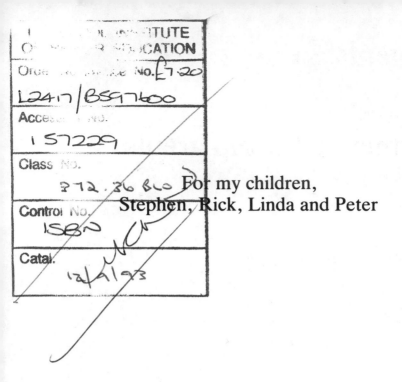
For my children,
Stephen, Rick, Linda and Peter

British Library Cataloguing in Publication Data

Bloom, Wendy
  Partnership with parents in reading.—
  (UKRA teaching of reading monographs)
  1. Reading (Elementary) 2. Parent-teacher relationships
  I. Title II. United Kingdom Reading Association
  III. Series
  372.4   LB1573
  ISBN 0-340-40215-6

First published 1987
Second impression 1989
Copyright © 1987 Wendy Bloom

Typeset by Rowland Phototypesetting Ltd,
Bury St Edmunds, Suffolk
Printed and bound in Great Britain
for Hodder and Stoughton Educational
a division of Hodder and Stoughton Ltd,
Mill Road, Dunton Green, Sevenoaks, Kent by
Biddles Ltd, Guildford and King's Lynn

Contents

Acknowledgments

I would like to thank the following people for their part in this book: Colin Harrison, the Series Editor, for his sound advice and guidance; Barry Stierer, not only for his permission to report extensively on his project 'Parental Help With Reading in Schools', but also for his time and generosity in sharing the process of the research; Annie Sevier and Ann Haines for the opportunity to work in their schools and to present case studies of their work with parents (see Chapters 3 and 8); Gordon Wells for permission to reproduce the exchange between mother and child in Chapter 2 from *Language, Learning and Education*; Ian Wilson, on behalf of SE Coventry Community Education Project for permission to use the 'Food' Home-Learning Pack and for his help and interest; Alan Roberts, for his help and encouragement and for giving me the opportunity to develop my interest in parental involvement in children's reading; Dermot Murphy, Senior Lecturer at St Mary's College, Strawberry Hill, for taking all the photographs reproduced in this book; all the many parents, teachers and children who have patiently and willingly given their time for discussion and answering questions; all the friends and colleagues in the Midlands and more recently in South London who have offered support and encouragement; Fiona Wray, Desk Editor at Hodder and Stoughton, who I am sure has done much more than usual in putting the book into shape; lastly, and not least, my husband, Malcolm, for his continuing encouragement without which I would never have completed this book.

Introduction

'I can't really spare the time to run a home-reading scheme, I would rather spend that time listening to children read.'

'If you let parents into the classroom, they'll just take over.'

'Our parents aren't bothered anyway – you can never get them to come into school.'

Variations on these comments are voiced every time that teachers meet together and discuss the theme of collaboration with parents over children's reading either at home or in school. Now the overwhelming force of evidence both from experimental projects and everyday working schemes points to the positive short and long-term benefits that can be gained.

'I would rather spend the time listening to children read.' Infant teachers, particularly, are rightly preoccupied with children's reading. They see reading as being crucial to children's progress in learning and indeed for their life opportunities. Parents see this too, not for all children, as teachers do, but for their own child. The question is, what is the best, most effective way of furthering children's reading – not in the mechanics of decoding but in a way that will help children to enjoy and use their reading at every opportunity. If we look at recent thinking about the reading process written by, for example, Frank Smith or Margaret Meek, we find that it follows naturally that other adults besides the teacher will need to be involved with children in their reading.

Both Frank Smith and Margaret Meek see the young child coming to reading as an apprentice reader and as such needing an adult as a guide. As Frank Smith states in *Reading* (1978): 'Two basic necessities for learning to read are the availability of interesting material that makes sense to the learner and an understanding adult as a guide.'

Margaret Meek reiterates this view in *Learning to Read* (1982): 'To learn to read, children need the attention of one patient adult, or older child, for long enough to read something that pleases them both.'

This book aims to show that in one way and another parents have a vital part to play in that process.

'If you let parents into the classroom, they'll just take over.' This kind of comment comes up mainly in middle-class areas and is directed at parents who might seem too assertive. The vast majority of teachers who do invite parents into the classroom find these fears are unfounded.

This book aims to describe and analyse various ways in which parents and teachers have worked successfully together in school to the benefit of every child's reading.

This book also sets out unashamedly to convince readers that collaboration with parents in children's reading is well worth while. Most teachers now have heard or read about the various projects and schemes, some of which are described in this book. Most teachers in infant schools allow or encourage children to take books home. The next step from this is to structure the practice and set up good communication with parents. Perhaps this book will help them to avoid some of the pitfalls if they start a scheme. Many teachers who have already begun a partnership with parents, based either at home or in school, will be interested in reading about other teachers' work, looking at issues and principles that are becoming evident and also placing their practice in the context of past and current research and thinking.

The whole practice of involving parents as partners in children's learning is not by any means without its problems. In an area of education where teachers are beginning to expand their normally defined role, where parents are being invited to participate at a time of economies in education, there are obvious social and political factors to be considered alongside educational issues. The evidence, however, is becoming incontrovertible and we seem to be entering a second phase in the movement. Over the last few years while some experimental projects such as those in Haringey, Belfield, Coventry and Hackney have been carried out and reported, many other teachers have been working with parents because they can see that it makes good sense. Now seems a good time to take stock of what has happened and what is happening, to see how schemes could be refined, and how projects could be initiated with greater chances of satisfaction to all concerned. This kind of work carries with it some risks and we need to be convinced that the outcome is likely to be worth the effort in time, thought and energy, because in education, as in other areas of endeavour, attention given in one direction is necessarily diverted from another.

A fairly accurate picture of the arguments for and against involving parents at home and in school is drawn in the following list, compiled from work with groups of teachers and parents.

FOR . . . in school

1   Teachers attempting to follow an holistic view of reading will be greatly helped by having other experienced readers available to read with children.
2   Children have more opportunity to read aloud and to share books with an interested adult.
3   Children are often motivated to read with adults other than their teacher and benefit simply from having an adult to read with individually.
4   Children can see parents and teachers co-operating together. This helps to minimise any conflict between home and school.

5 Parents who are involved in this way develop a better understanding of the reading process, the role of the teacher and, perhaps, of other areas of the curriculum.
6 Parents' expectations of their own child tend to become more realistic.
7 Parents often realise that their child is far more independent than he or she appears to be at home.

FOR . . . at home

1 Time spent in shared reading can cement the bond between parent and child.
2 Taking books home and reading with parents helps children to view reading as a means of relaxation and enjoyment rather than as just a school activity.
3 Reading with parents at home can lead to a real dialogue between parent and teacher about all aspects of the child's progress in school.
4 For children whose parents rarely come into school, a structured home-reading scheme can help to bring these two aspects of a child's life closer together.

FOR . . . in school and at home

1 Parents and teachers can keep in touch with each other.
2 Parents' knowledge of children's literature can be widened.
3 Teachers can be kept informed of aspects of children's lives that are important to their learning at school.
4 Teachers can learn to appreciate the special expertise of parents.
5 Parents and teachers can develop mutual respect and understanding through collaboration.

AGAINST . . . in school

1 Voluntary help can disguise the need for more teachers in times of economic stringency and affect employment prospects for teachers.
2 There may be a risk of breach of confidentiality.
3 Over-assertive parents may pose a threat to some teachers.

AGAINST . . . at home

1 Pressure or inappropriate responses to children's efforts may produce undue anxiety.

AGAINST . . . in school and at home

1 The activity of reading aloud should mainly be for diagnosis – parents may not be qualified for this role.
2 Overemphasis on reading aloud when the child has reached a stage of some fluency may slow down rather than enhance progress towards independence in reading.

The odds definitely seem to weigh down heavily on the side of parent-teacher partnership although there are obviously potential difficulties.

ABOUT THIS BOOK

The book aims to present balanced descriptions of successful experimental projects, background research, typical 'everyday' working collaboration, discussion of underlying issues and an historical perspective in which to set this current movement. It is an effort to present as wide a picture as is possible in one book, a picture that is persuasive but at the same time realistic. Section II is concerned with the different ways in which parents and teachers can collaborate within a home-reading scheme. Section III looks at parent and teacher collaboration in school. In more detail:

Chapter 1 discusses the history of the increasing interest in and concern about the influential and even vital role of parents in their child's education. Parents' role in schools and, more specifically, in their child's reading is traced. Recent projects that have become well-known are described and common threads are drawn together.

Chapter 2 describes the part parents play in young children's language development, with reference to recent research. There is a description and discussion of children's early reading experiences and how schools and teachers might encourage parents of pre-school children in their important role.

Chapter 3 deals with the infant school. It starts with a countdown to the start of a home-reading scheme and goes on to explore and develop the factors that must be considered if a scheme is to be successful.

Chapter 4 describes an experimental home-reading project in first schools which was set up on the strength of the Haringey Project. It aims to build up a real picture of small-scale research where many things do not turn out as intended.

Chapter 5 develops the argument from Chapter 4, tracing a group of the children as they move from a first to a middle school and indicating how their parents are still involved, but in different ways, as many of the group are by now fluent readers.

Chapter 6, while dealing mainly with the theme of children with reading difficulties, looks firstly at the two contrasting models of reading, the 'skills' and the 'process' models. There then follows a description of paired reading, together with a look at what is known as the Derbyshire Project.

Chapter 7 looks at how parents can be involved in working with teachers in school. The chapter is mainly concerned with describing and analysing the recent research carried out by Barry Stierer at the London Institute of Education.

Chapter 8 presents some descriptions of parents working in the classroom, both in the usual role of reading with children and also in less common ways – referring to the workshop approach at Foxhill and the parents-as-authors scheme in Inner London.

Chapter 9 offers a checklist for those starting to work in partnership with parents, and examines how teachers and intending teachers might be helped in preparing themselves for working with parents, while the concluding chapter summarises the aims of the book and looks forward to continued partnership between parents and teachers, in areas other than reading.

SECTION I

1 Setting the scene – an historical perspective

Why do teachers need to know about the historical perspective of parental involvement and some of the more recent research? Why can't they just get on with what they are doing if it seems to work well, and concentrate on the practical aspects of collaborating with parents?

Most importantly, teachers are professionals, which implies that they should know something about the 'why' as well as the 'how'. Theory and practice inform each other and it must always be so, otherwise we could just apprentice BEd students to the nearest practising teacher in the classroom and let them learn by imitation. The more well-informed and knowledgeable teachers are, the better they will be able to do their job in its wider terms and the more they will be able to question practice that evolves from theory, and theory that comes from analysing practice.

WHERE DID IT ALL START?

When tracing the recognition of the importance of parental influence on children's education, a good place to start is with J. P. Douglas and his longitudinal study of children from 1964–1968 written up in *The Home and the School* (1964) and *All our Future* (1968). In the latter Douglas writes: 'The child's capacity to do well at his work in school is to a certain degree dependent on the encouragement he gets from his parents.'

Douglas's research led him to conclude that middle-class parents showed more interest in their child's education than working-class parents, with the gap becoming more pronounced as the child's schooling progressed. Even more importantly, he found that the factor of parental interest was still 'considerable' after compensating for standard of home, family size and academic record of school.

The Plowden Report, *Children and their Primary Schools* (1967), starts to point the way forward in closing the gap. 'Many manual workers and their wives already encourage children in their efforts to learn. If there are many now, there can be even more later.' The report reflects on the theory that it is parental concern and attitude towards schools and education in general that is the biggest factor in predicting children's success at school. Looking at underlying influences which shape such attitudes, the report states: 'Our evidence suggests that parents' occupation, material circumstance and education explain only about one-quarter of the variation in attitudes, leaving three-quarters unaccounted for. This implies that attitudes could be affected in other ways and altered by persuasion.'

WHAT WERE SCHOOLS DOING?

Obviously, the 'persuasion' referred to in the Plowden Report is to come from schools. The report looked at the organisation for parent-teacher relations in some primary schools. It makes reference to the general satisfaction of the heads of schools in the survey about their arrangements. The survey team repeatedly received comments like, 'we have very good relations with parents', no matter how rudimentary their arrangements in fact were. *What is a good relationship with parents? criteria.*

Schools came in for a good deal of criticism about their alleged lack of enthusiasm in forging links with parents. In *Parents and School* J. Sallis alleges: '. . . some of them (schools) seem to want it (communication with parents) in the way the drunk wants a lamp-post – he's glad of the support but not so keen on the illumination!' More specifically she states: 'Parents are continually being told that their support is absolutely vital to their child's success and yet they are given no real role to play in a process in which their involvement is compulsory and their investment unique.' The recent movement towards collaboration in children's reading would certainly answer this allegation.

One of the reasons for the seeming reluctance of schools in the past (and of some schools now) to involve parents in a real way is put forward by J. Freeman in *In and Out of Schools* (1976). She writes: '. . . schools who fear that by opening the door a crack, the status of the teacher will drop, can have very little faith in their own expertise, and it is likely that this attitude will be apparent in greater rigidity and control in the school system.'

No survey of the state of relations between parents and schools would be complete without reference to Eric Midwinter. In *Education for Sale* (1977) he refers to 'the myth of parental apathy' . . . 'Teachers have blamed parents for being lethargic rather than themselves for being insensitive and insufficiently gifted in public relations.' Elsewhere in the book he writes: 'The idea that the child is taught solely and completely in school must be abandoned under the weight of fresh knowledge of the last fifteen years.'

It would seem that in the early 1970s schools were somewhat ambivalent in their attitude towards parents, on the one hand professing their concern to have good contacts with parents, and on the other hand often not setting up the machinery to enable it to happen. Similarly, on the one hand schools were exhorting parents to take more interest in their child's education, and on the other hand not opening specific channels through which this could be effected.

A major report which was drawn up in the latter part of the 1970s looked at the influence that parents might have in schools. This report (the Taylor Report) will now be considered in some detail because it is having, and will continue to have, far-reaching implications, and is likely to be a focus of discussion for some years to come.

Comments and criticisms were being voiced on the way in which schools related to parents. At this time (1975–77) the position of governing bodies in primary and secondary schools was being studied. Subsequently a report was compiled and recommendations made. The Taylor Report, *A New Partnership for our Schools*, was published in 1977 and had quite far-reaching implications for the relationship between parents and schools, the framework for the existing arrangements having been set up in the 1944 Education Act.

The part of the report that is concerned with parents is the recommendation that there should be an equal number of parents, school staff, LEA representatives and representatives from the local community in the governing body of each school. This would mean that one-quarter of each body would be comprised of parents, who would be elected by other parents. Both the elected parents and the parents who elect them must have a child currently at the school.

The report stressed that the fact of having one-quarter representation on the governing body does not in itself guarantee a satisfactory level of parental involvement in a school. It recommended that, in addition, 'parents' organisations should be encouraged and facilities for their work should be made available within the school'.

Governing bodies were urged to ensure that adequate arrangements are made so that individual parents can be involved in their children's progress and welfare. Another recommendation was that every parent should receive a written communication setting down information about the school – the aims, organisation and school rules. The compilation and distribution of the school brochure or booklet did not become mandatory until 1980 when recommendations in the Taylor Report were incuded in the 1980 Education Act. The proportional representation of parents on the school governing body was also made law in this Act.

INFLUENCE ON THE CURRICULUM

The Taylor Report also sought to extend the role of parents by extending the role of the governing body, particularly in decisions concerning the curriculum of the school. There is an interesting section in the report which looks back in time at the responsibilities of governing bodies in schools. The 1861 Clarendon Commission recommended that choice of subjects and any change in the curriculum should be the responsibility of the governors, while how to teach should be the responsibility of the head.

The Taunton Commission appointed in 1864 made a memorable comment about the place of parents: '. . . judicious parents when they have once reposed confidence in a headmaster never do interfere. They are nevertheless subject to all the evils resulting from interference of other parents more ignorant than themselves.'

Coming back up to date, the Taylor Report recommends that the newly-constituted governing body '. . . should be given by the LEA the responsibility for setting the aims of the school, for considering the means by which they are pursued, for keeping under view the school's progress towards them, and for deciding upon action to facilitate such progress.'

Government Green Paper: *Parental Influence at School*

This discussion document, published in 1984, seems to change the proportional representation of parents on school governing bodies. An example is given of the governing body of a typical primary school of 100–299 children. In such a school it is proposed that there should be 11 members. Of these, one would be the head, one a teacher, 6 would be parents and 3 LEA representatives.

The responsibilities of the governing body, with its majority made up of parents, would be as follows: within the LEA's curriculum policy framework to determine the 'range and pattern of the school's curriculum'. The organisation and delivery of that curriculum would be left to the head and teachers. The governing body would also be responsible for the 'conduct' of the school. This, generally speaking, would mean that, in consultation with the head, the governors would be responsible for a continuous appraisal of just about everything that went on in school, from methods of teaching to school uniform.

Since the time of the Green Paper it has become evident that parents generally are reluctant at the moment to take on such a heavy responsibility, so the fate of the proposals contained in the Green Paper is uncertain.

PARENTS AND READING

Having given general consideration to the picture in the late 1960s and early 1970s, it is now time to focus specifically on reading. The underlying reason for the concern to involve all parents with reading comes out in the national child development study of children from birth to seven, *Perspectives on School at Seven Years Old* by J. and E. Newson, published in 1977. In this study there was clear evidence of the relationship between social class and reading attainment. In the study's 'Competence in Reading Survey' it was found that while only 13% of children with fathers in social classes I and II were classified as poor readers, 48% of children with fathers in social class V were so classified. So children of unskilled manual workers were nearly four times more likely to experience difficulty with reading than the children of professional fathers.

In the same survey, the Newsons state that the majority of working-class parents were trying to help their children with reading. They write '. . . that over 80% of our sample claimed in fact to have given help with reading would suggest that, in their varying ways, most parents see themselves as having some part to play in this basic aspect of their child's education'. They go on to add '. . . and yet this willingness is too often mischannelled for lack of advice, encouragement and appreciation from those best qualified to give it'. They sum up '. . . schools are surely not only failing dismally in their educative role, but wasting the most valuable resource they have'. '*A revolution in literacy could be sparked off and fuelled by parents and teachers in determined co-operation*' (author's italics). Whether the current movement is going to bring about a revolution in literacy is debatable, but perhaps a quiet revolution is gathering momentum – and not only in literacy.

LOOKING AT PARENTAL INVOLVEMENT IN A WORKING-CLASS AREA

In the Plowden Report and in the survey written up by the Newsons, it was indicated that many working-class parents were trying to help their children with reading. In 1976, Jenny Hewison investigated the differences in reading attainment in a group of seven- and eight-year-old children in a working-class population in Dagenham, London. She carried out a series of three studies using standardised tests and parental interviews. After concluding the studies, she established that the factor in the child's home background which related most strongly to reading achievement was whether or not the mother regularly heard the child read. There seemed to be many factors that might be associated with success in reading: parental attitudes, a high IQ, a favourable language environment, help with reading at home, parents who were enthusiastic readers. In one study, the Wechsler Intelligence Scale for Children (WISC) scores were obtained, but it was shown that IQ differences did not account for the superior reading performance of the 'coached' group. It was also established that maternal language was not a significant factor. When the amount of coaching the children received was related to the reading test score, a highly significant positive association was found. Although the sample was relatively small (some 300 children) and drawn from a single area, there seemed to be a strong relationship between parental help at home and improved reading performance.

These were quite startling findings, showing that if working-class mothers regularly listened to their child read, this would appear to have a significant influence on their reading attainment.

Two questions emerged from the studies:

1 Why did some mothers listen to their children read and some not? It might have been the parents' general interest in education that led them to hear their child read regularly and this interest might have brought about better teaching. It may also have been that children who were better readers attracted more help from home.

2 Would the same improvement in reading result if *all* mothers in working-class families regularly listened to their child read?

THE HARINGEY PROJECT

If improved reading performance could be obtained by involving mothers, then this practice might well compensate for the difference in performance between the children from professional and working-class families reported in *Perspectives on School at Seven Years Old*.

Running concurrently with this series of studies was the Haringey Reading Project (1976–7), which aimed to show whether or not, when *all* parents were involved in a home-reading scheme, such considerable gains would still be achieved. Furthermore, as Jenny Hewison's studies had been conducted in an area where English was the mother tongue, could reading gains be achieved by children who came from families where there was little or no English spoken or read?

It is worth giving this project more than a passing mention, partly because of the wide publicity it received for its somewhat startling results, and also because it seems to have been a watershed in the movement to involve parents. There were many similar projects set up by individual teachers, by schools and by LEAs as a result of these findings, the project described in Chapter 4 being one example.

The purpose of the Haringey experiment was to try to establish if there was a causal relationship between active parental help in reading and children's reading performance.

The design of the Haringey Project

The project was based on three groups, based on classes in six infant schools in the borough of Haringey. It was not judged feasible or ethical to have split-class groups.

Group 1:   Two intervention class groups of six to seven year-olds based in two different schools.

Group 2:   Two small withdrawal groups from within two classes of six to seven year-olds based in two different schools – to receive help from a remedial teacher four times weekly.

Group 3:   Six control class groups based in each of the six schools.

There was random allocation of class groups to these three categories.

Duration: The intervention was planned to last two years.
Evaluation: Standardised reading tests were to be carried out at 4 different stages
   (a)   pre-intervention;
   (b)   after one year of intervention;
   (c)   post-intervention;
   (d)   12 months after the conclusion of the experiment.

Qualitative and illuminative data were also to be collected.

Method

Children from the two intervention classes were to take books home regularly, i.e. 2/3 times weekly. From these books they would read aloud to parents a passage allocated by the teacher. Parent and teacher were to use report cards to monitor reading and add comments.

The researchers, one for each class, were to contact parents at home and support and monitor reading at home throughout the project, and also to foster good contacts between parents, schools and teachers.

No attempt was to be made to inhibit any current practice of reading at home in non-intervention groups; therefore any positive results would be a conservative estimate of improvement.

Organisational and implementational questions to be answered through the Project

1 Is it feasible for *all* children?
2 Will children return books?
3 Will parents adopt the attitude that it is the school's obligation to provide all learning experiences required by children?
4 Will parents intervene in an inappropriate or punitive way?
5 Can non-English speaking or illiterate parents join the project?
6 Will this help lead to improved reading performance?

Results

Statistical analysis

At the conclusion of the first year of intervention the children in the home-intervention group had a higher mean reading score than the other groups, but it only reached a significant level in one school. After two years of intervention it was significant in both home-intervention schools. In the follow-up tests the significant gains were retained by one school, but although gains were sustained by the second school their level dropped to below a significant level.

Neither the withdrawal nor the control groups made significant gains over and above the expected chronological gains in the standard reading tests.

The gains made by the home-involvement groups were across the whole reading attainment range.

Qualitative data

1 Support for the project was high and there was a willingness for contact at home.
2 Parents welcomed advice.
3 Hardly any parents were using punitive measures during the practice of reading at home.

4 Parents responded better to unobtrusive demonstration than to explanations.

5 Parents with very little education themselves proved to be excellent in a collaborative role.

6 Parents spoke more fluent English at home than when they communicated with teachers at school.

7 There was negligible loss or damage to books.

8 The children seemed to be more autonomous in their reading, more highly motivated and more satisfying to teach.

9 The project was effective with illiterate and non-English speaking parents.

So the question 'Can all children, irrespective of social class or ethnic background achieve better results in reading if they are heard regularly at home?' received the answer 'Yes! they could', and what was more, the gains on the test scores were higher than those from the 'remedial' groups.

Other results were also encouraging; parents' and teachers' attitudes were enthusiastic and other classes in the schools soon became similarly involved. School-based lending libraries were set up. Teachers felt that some children showed more enthusiasm for their work at school and showed improved performance in other areas of the curriculum.

In his report to the DES, W. Schofield sums up the project:

The collaboration gave structure to an activity which the children might have performed on their own initiative. It was an activity which parents could encourage and supervise; an activity on which the teacher herself could offer advice, and there was immediate reward for the children as they progressed and learnt to read. Parents made it clear that they felt their own involvement to be important and rewarding, and so did the teachers.

THE BELFIELD READING PROJECT

Of course, the Haringey Project was not the only one going forward at this time. Another notable project described in *The Belfield Reading Project* was being carried out in Rochdale. It was started in 1978. The project was based on the practice of parents listening to their child read for a short time every night. Initially the target group was five-year-old children. The ingredients of the project included a comment card going between home and school, meetings with parents and home-visits by teachers.

Belfield is a Community school and had, prior to the project, built up good relationships with parents and the surrounding community. The local public library was situated within the school site. This obviously gave scope for various initiatives with reading. During the school holidays, while the home-reading scheme was running, books and record cards were transferred to the library so that the scheme could be continued through the holidays in a modified form. This was an important factor, especially with beginning readers.

The description so far might appear to imply an ideal background and setting for a proposed parent-teacher partnership on reading, but this was not so. Paul Whilby, reporting on the project for *The Sunday Times*, writes: 'If ever there was a school where you would expect to find the feckless, apathetic parent of popular myth, ignorant about and uninterested in his child's progress, Belfield is it.' In spite of the poor housing and high unemployment in the area, the project was to prove a success and an inspiration for teachers in schools similarly situated.

An integral part of the project was the element of home-visiting, usually carried out by the project coordinator. The importance of talking with parents at home is brought out again in Chapters 4 and 5. As Jackson and Hannon, authors of the report on the Project, state: 'We think that being prepared to talk to every parent personally plays an important part in the success of the scheme. Home visits mean that we can be in contact with all parents, not just those who can come to school or attend meetings.' When the project was described in *The Belfield Reading Project* in 1981 it had been running, expanding and developing for three years. For more fluent readers, other tasks were developed, but always with the parents occupying a central rather than subsidiary role.

HACKNEY PACT (PARENTS, CHILDREN AND TEACHERS)

This project has been described in two publications – a handbook for teachers entitled *Home-School Reading Partnerships in Hackney* (ILEA Pitfield Project, 1984) and also in *Parent, Teacher, Child* (Griffiths and Hamilton, 1984). The project was set up in Hackney in 1979 and comprised various different schemes operated by junior and infant schools together with some secondary schools within the borough. They were all based on co-operation with parents in home-reading schemes. The basis of the schemes was for younger children to read two or three times a week with their parents, for older children to read by themselves, and for a comment sheet to provide a regular means of communication between home and school.

The results from the various schemes have not been quantified in the same way as were those from the Haringey experiment. The reports do show, however, that as well as achieving gains in reading, the children concerned have developed more positive attitudes towards reading, and the commitment of teachers in the schools involved is well expressed. A closer liaison and mutual regard between parents and teachers has developed. Some of the schools have widened the concept of partnership to welcome parents into the classroom to participate in reading activities. The children read many more books, and as a consequence of the home-reading scheme the whole structure of the school literacy policy has been revised.

The accounts bring out very clearly the need for good humour, patience and perseverance on the part of the teachers (and presumably the parents) involved. They describe the shared satisfaction and pleasure of parents and teachers on behalf of the children as they gain in confidence and their reading 'takes off'. The reports also show that meticulous attention has to be given to maintaining good contacts over long periods of time – a factor that will be returned to in later chapters.

Again, like Haringey and Belfield, Hackney has a relatively small proportion of articulate middle-class parents. Most schools represent a racial and ethnic mix and many adults are unemployed. Parents in these areas often do not own very much in the material sense, but they do have something that is invaluable for their child's education: a unique concern for their own child and their own child's learning. When structured schemes can be set up and run and teachers can whole-heartedly share the responsibility of children's learning to read, then this natural concern can be channelled into something definite and dynamic for all three participants in the partnership.

The home-reading arrangement in each classroom in each school tends to be unique and have its own flavour. This must be so as it reflects the individuality of the class teacher and her response to the task as she sees it. There are, however, underlying factors that all arrangements have in common. They seem to be as follows:

1   Initial and long-lasting commitment and enthusiasm on the part of the teacher.
2   A deep conviction that all parents have an important part to play as educators – that not all learning takes place within school.
3   Efforts to involve all children are made; this includes willingness to meet parents at home as well as in school to start the scheme.
4   Good, regular contact with parents while the scheme is in progress, to advise and guide and to encourage, praise and support – in fact an extension of teachers' professionalism into a new area.
5   The provision of a wide selection of good books that children and parents want to read. This is where LEAs or any other agency with the necessary finance are needed.
6   A clear idea of what is being aimed for and a willingness and capacity to reflect on whether such aims are becoming or have become realised.
7   Flexibility and hard work (the added workload requires reorganisation of other parts of the curriculum and a creative use of time)

SUMMARY

This chapter has attempted to look at three aspects of parental involvement:

1   To trace the growing interest and concern in the influence of parents on their child's education, and also, since the Taylor Report, on what goes on in schools;

2   to look at the research into ways in which parents through all socio-economic groups were, on their own initiative, trying to help their children with reading;

3   to describe three reading projects where parents and teachers have collaborated successfully. Apart from the benefits to the children, these projects have helped to dispel the myth that working-class parents are uninterested or unable to help with their children's learning.

SECTION II

This section of the book concentrates on the parent and child reading together at home. Following on from Chapter 2 – which looks at the language experience of the pre-school child – Chapters 3, 4 and 5 are concerned with case studies and typical ways of collaborating with parents in home-reading/learning schemes.

2   The pre-school child

EARLY TALK

There has been a great deal of interest generated in the mid 1980s in the early talk of children and in their reading experiences at home. Links are being made between certain kinds of language activities at home and subsequent progress in school.

Before children come to school they are taught, or more accurately, they learn, very many things from their parents. The most important thing they learn to do, as far as education is concerned, is to talk, to use language. Teachers, psychologists and psycholinguists are all preoccupied with children's early language development. This concern is different, in part, from that of parents; they see their child's talk primarily as a means of communication. Others see it as a tool for thinking and reasoning and also more particularly, as far as this chapter is concerned, as a precursor to successful reading.

The work of Gordon Wells and others at Bristol University is prominent amongst the recent research into early language development. His longitudinal study of children across all social groups showed the particular ways in which parents can affect the development of language. The recent work and writings of Tizard and Hughes (1984), Margaret Meek (1985) and Margaret Clark (1976) also inform and illuminate this area of concern, and we shall consider their research later in this chapter.

Gordon Wells' study of oral language development is reported in *Language Learning and Education* and *Language and Learning*. One such study showed that the richer and more prolonged conversations, which provided most opportunity for learning, took place between mother and child, and came from shared everyday activities around the home. At these times, children are not only learning from their mother about life, people, and how things work, but also about language itself. Equally, the more they learn about language through conversation with their mother, the more they can *use* that language to find out even more about life, people and how things work.

Wells writes that '. . . the most effective talking and learning will take place when adults and children engage together in an *apprenticeship in meaning*. They should treat the child as a conversational partner who has something interesting to say and they should support his attempts to communicate and extend his contributions. By contrast, an adult style of conversation which is dominating and didactic is not helpful to a child of this age.'

The idea that the home can be the very best context for oral language development across all social classes, is reinforced by B. Tizard and M. Hughes in their book, *Young Children Learning*. In their study of the verbal interactions of a group of four-year-old girls they compared and contrasted the context of home with that of nursery schools and classes. They found that the highest quality of interaction, producing the most opportunities for cognitive development, was between mother and child at home.

They summarised the reasons for this conclusion by isolating five factors which emerged from the research:

1 At home there was an extensive range of activities; these included cooking, cleaning, planning shopping, budgeting and visits to and from other adults. There were very many opportunities for learning.
2 Mother and child shared a life which had a common past and future. The mother could extend the 'here and now' for the child, back into the past and forward into the future, as no other adult could. Their shared experience formed the basis for summary and conjecture – two cognitive strategies essential to any form of learning.
3 In the home there are only a small number of children who have to share the adult's time. Consequently there are more opportunities for prolonged, uninterrupted conversations.

There is the closest of relationships between mother and child.

4   The learning which took place was embedded in contexts which had great meaning for the child, and therefore the learning was likely to be retained and built upon.

5   There is the closest of relationships between mother and child. It is of great concern to the mother that her child should acquire certain educational skills. The emphasis that each mother places on the two main areas of learning, cognitive or social, varies with each family.

In their research Tizard and Hughes, like Wells, found that the context for effective conversation did not need to be educational. 'Effective' conversation usually has a recognisable pattern to it. It contains certain criteria:

(a)   The topic is initiated by the child.
(b)   The parent takes up the topic at the child's level.
(c)   The balance of questioning is usually fairly even between parent and child.
(d)   The parent tries to help the child extend the topic.
(e)   The parent provides a language model for the child.
(f)   The whole conversation provides mutual satisfaction.

Wells (1982) gives the following example of conversation between Mark (just over two years old) and his mother. Mark is looking out of the window and notices that a man who was making a bonfire has now gone. (The letters in brackets refer to the criteria listed above.)

Mark	Mother
Where man gone?	
Where man gone? (a)	I don't know.
	I expect he's gone inside
	because it's snowing. (b) (e)
Where man gone?	In the house.
Uh?	Into his house.
No.	
No.	
Gone to shop, Mummy.	Gone where?
(The local shop is close to Mark's house.)	
Gone shop.	To the shop? (e)
Yeh.	What's he going to buy? (d)
Er – biscuits.	Biscuits mm.
Uh?	Mm.
	What else? (d)
Er – meat.	Mm.

Meat.
Er – sweeties.
Buy a big bag sweets.   Buy sweets?

Yeh.
M – er – man – buy –
the man buy sweets.   Will he?

Yeh.
Daddy buy sweets.
Daddy buy sweets.   Why?

Oh, er – shop.
Mark do buy some – sweet –
sweeties.
Mark buy some – um.
Mark buy some – um.

I did.

This equal balance of conversation is difficult to reproduce in school. Often the teacher is concerned not only with the child's language development, but also with class control and shaping talk to specific ends.

Many parents seem to respond intuitively to children's talk in a way that extends the child's area of knowledge about the world and about language. Nursery and infant school teachers could perhaps find opportunities to confirm what those parents are already doing. For parents who, perhaps, do not see the need for protracted conversations, the simple idea of one long conversation per day being worth many short remarks could be useful and workable. The main aim, though, would be for teachers to raise parents' awareness of the importance of language and also emphasise to parents the value of what they do intuitively.

EARLY READING

Children do not *start* to read when they come to school. Almost all children have travelled some distance along the road to becoming a reader before formal education begins. Indeed, some children are already fluent readers by the time they are five. Margaret Clark describes some such readers vividly in *Young Fluent Readers*.

Infant teachers, especially reception class teachers, place great importance on children's early language development. They feel that before children can formally begin the process of learning to read they must have a certain 'level' of oral language. From Wells' study it seems that this emphasis may be misplaced. The results of the research seemed to indicate that oral language ability was not the main predictor of early reading success. They found that knowledge of, and interest in, literature was the highest predictor of later success in reading.

Wells used the Marie Clay tests which help the teacher to ascertain children's concepts about print. This is done through the teacher reading the test booklet with the child and asking specific questions about various concepts such as word order, directionality, letter order – in all 24 items which are scored.

He found that: 'The best single predictor of success in reading after two years in school was the knowledge about literacy the children already possessed on entry to school.'

A further piece of very interesting evidence emerged from the studies. It was found that familiarity with written language in extended prose (stories) before school seemed to be a high predictor of children's academic achievement in school at seven years old. To explain this link, Wells suggests that in order to meet the demands of formal education, children need to be able to disengage their thinking from immediate contexts of activity. They need to be able to think about real and hypothetical experiences through the medium of words alone. Stories, and all the talk that surrounds story-reading, give young children an important introduction to this powerful function of language.

Wells states that when young children share books with adults they can learn three things:

1 They can learn about how books work, and the language of book reading, such as 'page', 'word', 'letter', 'line'. They can also begin to recognise individual words and groups of words.

Research has shown what an important 'educational' role parents play before their child starts school.

2   Children can start to learn about how stories work. They can learn about the shape of stories, about characters and plot and relate imaginary events in books to their own lives, giving insights into both.

3   Most importantly, as mentioned before, children can learn to use langauge to think in a 'disembodied' way – removed from the 'here and now' and the physical context.

More recently, the same studies seem to be showing that the frequency with which young children are read to at home before starting school is a powerful predictor of later school success. As Wells explains, not only do children gain insight by relating imaginary events in books to their own lives, but also they learn that written language has the potential to create alternative 'possible worlds' through words.

WHAT CAN PARENTS DO BEFORE THEIR CHILD GOES TO SCHOOL?

Research has shown that parents play an important 'educational' role before their child starts school. It seems, from the results of the research and from using common sense, that the three best things parents can do are:

1   Recognise the importance of talk; that one long conversation a day around a topic that the child initiates is worth many brief questions and remarks; that when a child starts a conversation it is good to pick up from 'where the child is' and to carry on a bit further, both in language structures (syntax) and in meaning (semantics). Many, many parents do this instinctively and it would be presumptuous of teachers to try to 'teach' parents this. It would also tend to inject artificiality into situations that must be spontaneous to work properly. Perhaps, though, teachers could, with the aid of video and through discussion, share these kinds of strategies with parents and try to explain why they are so important.

2   Use the written language around us – know how important a source of reading it is. Without too much contrivance, children's attention can be drawn to all the different kinds of signs, notices, warnings, labels and advertisements around us. Particularly useful in this context are TV commercials because the words are seen at the same time as they are heard. They are presented in such a way, in a jingle or with emphasis, as to be readily memorable. Again, it would be condescending to 'teach' parents this, as they are already aware of it. The teacher's part is to raise awareness of the richness and importance of these sources of reading.

3   Make stories and rhymes a familiar part of children's early language experience. Margaret Meek in *Learning to Read* (a book aimed at parents but very good for teachers too), describes many sound ways and

good reasons for spending time on stories and rhymes. The earliest jingles and nursery rhymes are important for their rhythm, pattern of language and the intonation used in the telling. For stories to be important to a child's development they must grip and absorb the child, otherwise they are ineffective for this purpose.

SHOULD PARENTS TEACH CHILDREN TO READ BEFORE SCHOOL?

In the late 1970s this was a much debated question. Margaret Clark discusses it in her book, *Young Fluent Readers*, which is a study of thirty-two children from all social backgrounds who could read competently before coming to school. Some mothers in the survey said that they were apprehensive and embarrassed about informing reception class teachers that their child could read. Some teachers were, in fact, sceptical, and some mothers had actively tried to discourage their children who wanted to read for fear of the complications that might later arise.

Time was when a mother would 'confess' that her child could read, only to be told that that was as may be, but the child would have to toil through the pre-reading hurdles nonetheless – through the flash cards or the phonic exercises and on to the readers. Meanwhile, the mother was mentally marked down as being too pushy, and retired hurt! More importantly, children would be puzzled and confused by the whole process of learning to read at school, as it would often bear little resemblance to the more holistic approach instinctively followed at home.

The actual books used in school, the early readers, could present a problem to these children. These readers are based on a skills approach to reading where adults have determined that the best way to learn is by breaking down the text into its smallest components. Margaret Meek writes in *Language and Learning* (Wells and Nicholls, 1985) '. . . that children are not ready for Janet and John when entering school. Parents and teachers know the purposes and mechanics but real authors are needed to make the whole thing work . . . the effective texts say "suppose".'

A child could be puzzled and uncertain when confronted by flash cards, early phonics and sterile readers, and could end up by deciding to opt out of the whole affair – thus confirming the teacher's suspicion that the mother had vastly exaggerated her claims!

Fortunately, this picture does not exist in reception classes today most teachers are much more sensitive to parents as educators. A reception class teacher who has the responsibility of introducing thirty children to reading must be pleased when some of these children do not need such a high level of attention. Moreover, children who can and do read and who enjoy reading will provide models for the more inexperienced readers. They can also share their reading with their friends, talk about books, and recommend their favourites to other children.

HOW CAN TEACHERS HELP?

Teachers can help parents by introducing to them the many excellent books available for very young children, much better than the ones parents themselves experienced when they were young. Teachers can explain how books without texts like the Ormerods' *Moonlight* and *Sunshine* work. They can read with parents books like *Rosie's Walk*, by Pat Hutchins, which is a fine example of how text and illustrations work together, and how the reader and writer enter into a pact – as happens in all the best books.

The way in which young children approach reading before school is important. Teachers have the task of explaining to prospective parents that it is the meaning, excitement and enjoyment to be had from reading that promotes early success and makes children lifelong readers. The books which children start reading are vitally important and parents may need to be advised against urging their child through, for instance, the Ladybird Key Reading Scheme on display not only in bookshops, but also often in newsagents, chemists and supermarkets. Children need to start reading with real stories.

Teachers could try to explain to parents how young children can be looked upon as 'apprentice readers'. They can learn to read alongside an adult. They can be encouraged to join in the reading. Stories like *The Enormous Turnip* and *The Three Little Pigs* give marvellous opportunities for this, with repetitious passages that invite participation by the child. It is good for children to have the same story read to them over and over again. This gives young children the chance to predict successfully the unfolding of the story and also to make the story their own, part of their experience. Children of three and four can 'read' their favourite books which they know by heart, turning the pages as they tell the story.

Many infant schools have good links with their local playgroups and nurseries; many have a nursery class situated within the school. This is an ideal context in which to work with staff and parents. Some schools have set up mother and toddler libraries so that when mothers come to school they can borrow books for the younger members of the family. Again, this would be an ideal context for talk, discussion and demonstration about books and reading and how parents could help.

SUMMARY AND CONCLUSIONS

This chapter has been about the unique contribution that parents can make to their child's developing language, both in talk and in reading, before school. Recent research seems to show the richness of the home context for the most productive talk. There seems to be a causal link between young children's sharing of books with adults at home and their subsequent progress in reading and other areas of learning. Some ways in which teachers might work with parents before their child starts school have been suggested.

3 Collaborating with parents in the infant school

In this chapter we turn to an infant school to look at some common ways of setting up and implementing a home-reading scheme.

The chapter starts with commentary notes showing how the idea of starting a home-reading scheme was developed but postponed until the whole school felt ready to implement a scheme based on the PACT collaboration in Hackney.

The school, in Outer London, had a very mixed intake which included children with Asian background and also children of temporarily homeless families. This is a timetable of events leading up to the start of the scheme:

1981–September
(new head in
school)

The deputy head reads about the Belfield project in *The Times Educational Supplement*, obtains further information and enthusiastically presents this to a staff meeting. Should the school initiate such a scheme? Some of the teachers have strong reservations – no decision is taken to institute a scheme.

1982–January

The school does resolve to involve parents but decides only to ask parents to write reports on the library books children have taken home. This idea never really 'catches on' and is dropped after a few months.

The idea of a pilot home-reading scheme is considered but rejected. The feeling is that the school should act together in this kind of collaboration.

Late 1982–
Early 1983

The head decides that reading and language work need urgent consideration. This has priority over any initiative on involving parents.

The reading schemes being used are Happy Venture, Breakthrough and Ladybird.

The LEA requirement for standardised testing uses the Schonell Word Recognition Test.

Many curriculum development meetings follow. The school starts to move towards a more holistic view of reading and away from a skills-based approach.

1984–September	A new deputy head and a postholder for language are appointed. The time seems right for another look at involving parents with reading.
1985–January	A series of meetings are held in school and a general consensus is obtained for starting a home-reading scheme. Information from the Hackey PACT project is obtained and discussed. The ILEA video of the project is borrowed from the LEA, watched and discussed. The head this time plays 'devil's advocate', helping to bring into the open points of reservation felt by some of the teachers.
1985–March to October	Planning for the home-reading scheme begins. There is no money for books so a Friday cake stall is instituted with teachers and parents supplying and buying for 'books to send home'. A home-reading logo is developed and stuck onto each book purchased.

At this time the LEA Educational Psychologist is co-ordinating a paired-reading scheme – involving parents and children from some schools in the borough. The school does not take part but takes an interest in the project.

The LEA provides money for new and more appropriate 'core' reading materials.

Teachers visit a nearby school which has adopted the Hackney PACT scheme.

Many staff meetings are held to discuss organisation, books and communication with parents.

Teachers compile their own guidance and advice booklet for parents and their own comment sheets, both with the home-reading logo. They decide always to use pink paper when communicating with parents about the scheme.

The LEA provides help with reprographics.

All books are colour-coded according to the stages in *Individualised Reading* by Cliff Moon.

More money is now needed to purchase wallets and other stationery so a jumble sale is held.

A publicity board is put up for parents in the entrance hall.

1985–October	All the teachers attend a meeting of the National Association for Primary Education to promote the case for parental involvement in reading. They return to school enthusiastic and ready to begin.

1985–November   Initial meetings with parents are to be held in year groups with two teachers running the meeting between them. The main aim is to show parents how books work, so teachers read and share books with the parents. Enjoyment and shared reading are emphasised. A translator helps at some meetings. Guidance booklets are distributed and comment sheets explained.

The next day the children of the parents who have attended the meetings choose their first books to take home and are provided with a plastic wallet in which to keep the book.

Most classes are operating a once-a-week schedule to start with. Teachers begin trying to contact parents who did not attend meetings.

1985–December   Already feedback is coming in from parents, and teachers have much to discuss.

There is a general feeling of relief that the scheme is under way without too many problems having arisen.

Plans are discussed for making sure that all parents are contacted.

Consideration is given as to how many times a week home-reading will take place.

Special arrangements for individual children and parents are being thought about.

Another meeting, at which part of the PACT video will be shown to parents, is being considered.

THE HOME-READING SCHEME IN THE INFANT SCHOOL

In most schools the initiative for setting up a home-reading scheme will probably not have come from the LEA as it did in the project which will be described in Chapter 4, but rather from within the school – from the head, an individual teacher or a small group of teachers – as it was in the case described above.

It may well be that teachers are àlready sending 'reading' books home, and the school wishes to extend, formalise and structure this practice. The involvement of parents is in this way given a higher status and teachers, children and parents recognise its importance.

The movement towards involving parents in children's reading is, as we have seen, neither very new nor revolutionary, but it is a crucial step along a path which might now widen and even take a different direction as parents and teachers start to work together in partnership.

It might be useful to look at the different stages of planning and implementing a scheme, and to consider each stage in some detail. The whole process can be looked at in four main stages:

1 Thinking about and planning the scheme;
2 introducing the scheme;
3 implementing the scheme;
4 evaluating the scheme with a view to further development or change.

THE THINKING AND PLANNING STAGE

The idea of starting a home-reading scheme may have reached the school from various sources. It may have come from a neighbouring school or from in-service meetings. It may have come from reading the many and various articles in journals or the very informative books now being published about parental involvement. Many schemes have been set up as a direct result of projects such as Haringey and Belfield, and now PACT schemes are evolving as a result of the work in Hackney, particularly in boroughs around London. Teachers and researchers in these well-known projects are often invited to talk to groups of teachers who are interested in starting schemes in their own schools.

Who will start the scheme?

Given that someone in a school feels really strongly that they want to involve parents in children's reading, where do they start? It must depend somewhat on the position of the teacher in the school. The head or the deputy would have the power to arrange staff meetings and to inform and persuade other members of staff of the benefits to be gained. The language postholder in the school might be able to operate in a similar way, except that he/she would have to consult with the head and deputy first. The class teacher has a more difficult task and would probably enlist the help and interest of a colleague, who might be the postholder, before approaching the head and other members of staff.

Curriculum change – for this is what this is – comes about in many different ways, depending on the style of management in a school and the complexity of professional and personal relationships. The effects of change or development will obviously be more marked if there is whole-school consensus to act together. This consensus is well worth working for, even if, as in the case study summarised at the beginning of the chapter, it takes a long time to evolve.

The alternative to whole-school action is for one or two teachers to proceed with a scheme, perhaps in a pilot form, and report their experiences and findings to the rest of the school. Usually the most enthusiastic teacher will start, but it can happen that an age-group of children is chosen for the initial experiment. There is a case to be made for concentrating on each of the three age-groups in an infant school. In the reception class, parents are naturally very concerned about their child's transition from home to school. Involving reception class parents can help their children to make a good start with reading. In the middle age-group, children are gaining confidence with their reading and parents may feel more secure in their role as partner. Top infant class children's reading could be given a real boost before they move to junior school where, perhaps, reading is valued less for its own sake than for being a learning tool. At the same time, some children could be given emergency help. This would be a good time for intensified effort to help the few struggling readers to attain fluency and confidence.

Some individual teachers proceed with a scheme without the active support or interest of the rest of the school. This is not impossible but can be difficult and cause problems. The teacher who takes this course needs to make repeated and strenuous efforts to interest other colleagues. Sometimes in such cases parents who are involved, or who wish to be, try to influence other teachers to work in the same way. This can be counter-productive. However, a home-reading scheme is one enterprise where teachers can operate individually – albeit with much care and sensitivity – unlike other areas of the curriculum, where it would be impossible. For example, it would hardly be feasible for one teacher acting independently to introduce a separate maths scheme.

What are the school's aims in setting up a home-reading scheme?

What does the school hope will come out of such a scheme, for the children, parents, teachers and the school as a whole?

The first aim, clearly, is to affect the children's reading in some way, but in what way? Do we want children to read more; to read more fluently; with more understanding; to enjoy books and reading more? Do we want them to be more discriminating readers, to gain more confidence and independence in their reading? Do we want them ultimately to turn to reading readily and effectively for pleasure, satisfaction, to solve problems and follow their interests? On the other hand, our aims may be more in the way of better reading test scores or quicker progress through a reading scheme. This divergence of aims is to do with means and ends, which really reflects the model of reading to which a school subscribes. It is important that the teachers and schools make clear which model of reading they follow – a skills model or a process model. When this is done, schools can more easily identify their aims and can see more clearly where parents' contributions fit in and, of course, the better the explanation to parents, the closer the possible collaboration. A deeper and more detailed look at the two models of reading and their implications for involving parents is given at the beginning of Chapter 6.

The school's aims may not be confined to progress in reading. Teachers may see the collaboration between themselves and parents as being beneficial in other ways. One of the school's aims may be a better understanding and openness between parents and teachers, and between home and school. The partnership in reading and the value placed on parents' contributions may help further this aim. Children who sometimes experience a conflict arising from the differences between the values and attitudes of home and school can become more confident in all their activities in school when they see parents and teachers working together for their benefit.

Which books? Who will choose – teacher or child?

These questions must be answered before the scheme starts. It will almost certainly be necessary to purchàse more books and the school will have to decide what kind of books they will need. The decision as to which books will be taken home as part of the scheme depends on the way in which the school views reading. The choice will be between:

1   the 'main reader' from a reading scheme or a supplementary book within the scheme;
2   other structured books which are part of a reading series;
3   single 'real' books which are in a graded system, such as described in Cliff Moon's *Individualised Reading*;
4   any individual 'real' book.

These options may not be mutually exclusive and can be varied for different children for different reasons. If, though, the main purpose of the home-reading scheme is for extra practice, then it might be a 'reader' that is taken home. If accuracy is considered important, then the child might read a passage to the teacher in school, and re-read the same passage at home. This can prove a rather sterile experience.

While many schools store their books and code them according to a level of difficulty, others do not grade their books at all. They feel that the child as reader is the best judge of what is suitable for them at any one time. The teacher, in these cases, keeps a watching brief and a record of what the child chooses. Through their considerable knowledge of children's books and of individual children, teachers will discuss and recommend books.

The 'level of difficulty' or of 'complexity' depends very much on the content of the book, the full meaning that it carries, the concepts conveyed, the style of the writer, the predictability of the story and the language used. These factors in the book then react with the experiences, preferences, hopes, moods and attitudes of the reader at the time of reading. It is difficult to see how all these things can be quantified in any reliable way. Certainly the more subjective base of *Individualised Reading* is more realistic than the many and varied readability formulae that are so popular. Looking at the whole picture of reader and book logically, some of the early 'readers' may be far more 'difficult' than real books on account of the strange language, lack of story line and, consequently, little opportunity for the reader to predict or to become truly engaged with the text.

Many infant schools use a code to label books which children read with parents at home. They put different coloured markers or indicators to show:

1 This is a book your child would like read to him/her.
2 This is a book your child can read to you with a little help.
3 This is a book which is an old favourite and which your child wants to read again (and again – try to enjoy it!).

It is also at the planning stage that a bid for money to buy new books may have to be made. The school in the case study had a cake stall and efforts like this, involving parents, are possible. A contribution from an LEA contingency fund for curriculum renewal may be feasible. The school mentioned earlier received a grant for a new core reading scheme which related to their new initiative in reading. Schools should be advised that these occasional grants of money may be conditional and such implications should be examined carefully. Local firms, societies and shops could be approached. In the Bradford book flood – the experiment in reading described in *Books and Reading Development* by J. Ingham – various such sources were tapped in order to provide enough books.

Certainly, in any home-reading scheme, many more books will be read, so it is necessary to prepare for this in advance; otherwise the scheme could founder for want of a good, interesting and varied collection of books.

The storage and retrieval of books must be planned in advance. The school in the case study described earlier purchased book trays in two different colours for incoming and outgoing books. Some schools eke out resources by having half the class read with parents on two nights a week, and the other half on another two nights. For taking the books home, the zip-up plastic wallets are popular. These can be purchased more cheaply in bulk and can have the home-reading logo stuck on, together with the child's name. The logo itself needs designing. Some schools have a competition for this; in other schools a group of teachers or parents undertake the work. These are small, but important touches and all go to 'sell' the scheme by making the process more professional-looking and attractive.

How often should children and parents read together at home?

Projects vary in the frequency of the shared reading at home from once a week to every weekday evening. Reading together once a week, especially when children might have been taking a book home more often previously, seems a rather low target. It would be difficult to keep up a lively written exchange and the scheme might not have much impact. On the other hand, reading every evening can demand much teacher time taken in organising and writing on the comment sheets. Some schools who have a scheme like this are now seriously considering modifying this practice. Parents, too, comment that if they have more than one child in the scheme to read with every night, they do feel rather hard-pressed. Some parents confessed to reading with children at the breakfast table, or to the child reading to them in the car on the way to school! Reading together every evening may be right for a short time or for children who are experiencing difficulties (see Chapter 6 and the section on paired reading). So, on balance, it would seem that two or three times a week might well be a good level of frequency.

What guidance, advice or instruction should be offered to parents?

Parents do *not* need to be like teachers. They have a very different role to play in a home-reading scheme which is equal and complementary to that of the teachers. Their unique concern for their child and the provision of a relaxed home setting for shared reading is what makes their side of the collaboration so effective. It does seem, though, that the more teachers can express their view of reading to parents the more effective the collaboration. Most schools send letters of explanation and arrange meetings with, perhaps, a video and some role play.

First meeting

Schools need to decide very carefully on the content of their first meeting with parents, and in particular on how much explanation or guidance is to

Smaller numbers of parents mean that they feel easier about asking questions and making comments.

be given. The school must inform parents of its own model of reading. The school in the case study described earlier in the chapter prepared year and class meetings where they read to parents to show them how books work. If a small group of parents is involved, they may feel easier about asking questions and making comments – especially if there is a book display and a chance to talk informally over a cup of tea. If a large whole-school meeting is arranged, perhaps to listen to a well-known speaker on the subject, then certainly smaller meetings need to be arranged as well.

Teachers might want to prepare a 'put yourself in their place' approach. This can be quite light-hearted, with parents participating. Two useful sources of materials are a pack published by Coventry LEA and the Caper Kit, published in *Children and Parents Enjoying Reading* (Branston and Provis, 1986).

What needs to be shown at this meeting is the value of parents' contribution, the enjoyment and satisfaction to be had from reading, and how the school approaches reading with its children.

Printed guidelines

If the school is going to offer parents printed guidelines, they need to be prepared in advance. If the teachers decide to prepare their own booklet, it must be of a good standard graphically and must identify visually with the home-reading scheme. Such a production takes time and skill. Schools might look to their teachers' centre, a neighbouring secondary school, or to a local college of further or higher education where students might do this for them. There are quite a number of published booklets now available. The ILEA publication, *Read, Read, Read* (1984), is very comprehensive and readable. Shorter booklets can be purchased from The Centre for the Teaching of Reading and from the Community Education Development Centre in Coventry.

Communication between home and school

Parents and teachers need to maintain communication once the home-reading scheme has begun, and the methods need to be planned in advance. In the Hackney PACT scheme, teachers made themselves available on a certain evening each week, as well as for more immediate queries. Teachers also need to decide if they will visit parents at home during the project. As well as individual contacts, group follow-up meetings may be planned. These can encourage and sustain all concerned, as well as provide a venue for receiving feedback and sharing information.

Most home-reading schemes include the use of a comment sheet or card which encourages written communication between parents and teachers. There are published cards available from the CEDC in Coventry, but most schools prefer to produce their own. Comment cards will carry the logo for the home-reading scheme and will generally follow this pattern:

Date	Teacher	Parent

Fold

What approach should we take with parents whose mother tongue is not English?

In all the published and well-known home-reading projects it has been found that *all* parents can contribute effectively. It would certainly be wrong to exclude parents whose mother tongue is not English on this score, though special thought and provision may have to be made for them. There are two main alternatives for the actual reading at home in such circumstances:

1 The child reads to the parent in English. The parent sits with the child and gives encouragement. The child then talks about the book in the common language. This means that the book would have to be at a level where the child can read independently.
2 Another member of the family reads with the child.

Sometimes families use both these arrangements.

In these circumstances, a translator may be needed for an initial meeting and for any follow-up meetings. Also, the written communication between home and school may need to be translated into the parents' mother tongue.

What about parents who are not literate?

The same kind of procedure can operate here, but a great deal of sensitivity is needed on the part of the teacher. Sometimes these parents have very unpleasant memories of school and also they feel that they have very little to offer when it comes to their child's literacy. It does happen sometimes that non-literate parents, and also parents who do not have much English, are spurred on by this situation to join adult groups for help and instruction. The teacher's support and encouragement are much appreciated in these circumstances.

What should we do if some parents do not join the scheme?

At the planning stage, thought needs to be given to this contingency. Much depends on the amount of time the school can give to encouraging all parents to take part. Of course, parents cannot be required to take part. It may be that teachers could arrange to talk to parents at home with a fuller and more individual explanation of the scheme and its benefits for their child. The reasons that parents give for being unable or unwilling to join must be listened to sympathetically. Very occasionally it is unwise to try to persuade reluctant parents to co-operate. They may already be under pressure from another source and the addition of another source of anxiety could prove very counterproductive for both the child and the parent.

Reluctant parents have said that they eventually joined schemes because their child felt isolated. Obviously this is not a very good way to start and perhaps teachers might give extra support and encouragement to such children when the scheme is running smoothly. Both the school in the case study and some schools referred to in Chapter 7 used their parent-helpers to read with children who are not involved regularly in school in an effort to ameliorate their feelings.

Shall we try to evaluate the scheme – if so, how?

Although evaluation is mentioned as the fourth and last stage, the decision as to whether and how to evaluate the scheme belongs in the planning stage. The well-known published projects all carried some kind of standardised testing because of their essentially experimental nature. The main disadvantage of standardised tests is that their principal function is to distinguish between children's level of performance in the test rather than to reflect the complexity of the reading process. The results obtained are only a reflection of the child's response to a test that concentrates on certain aspects of reading in a test situation and does not necessarily reflect the way in which a child reads when absorbed in a book. If, however, the school perceives reading as a hierarchical set of skills, then perhaps such testing would be an indicator of change.

It might be more profitable to look for other indicators of progress in the direction in which the school is aiming. The written exchanges between parents and teachers on the comment card could be studied and an analysis attempted. Teachers could decide to keep a log book to record observations and comments made by children. In *Raising Standards* (1984), the report of the study in Coventry schools, the Hunter Grundin Test of Reading Attitudes was used. The number of books read could be recorded and used as an indicator, and so could the way in which children talked and wrote about the books they read. Increasing discrimination in choosing books might be looked for; how often children choose reading as a voluntary activity at school and at home; how children 'settle in' to the regular times with books.

Parents' responses should always be sought when monitoring progress. Taped discussions with individuals or groups of parents are a very useful source of information as to how a project is developing. Teachers should not worry that qualitative data is not objective. The reading process is different in each reader and the progress of a partnership in a scheme like this is made up of many *subjective* attitudes and feelings; they should try to tune into these and be guided by them.

It is evident that a considerable amount of planning is necessary before a project starts. The preceding factors need to be thought about and discussed. The success of a project probably depends to a great extent on the amount and quality of thought and preparation that has been invested. The following stages of the project have all been considered in the planning and just need a few additional comments.

INTRODUCING THE SCHEME

The initial contact with parents has been discussed in the previous section. All that is needed is to decide when the scheme should start. Many schemes are launched near the beginning of the school year. This is a good time psychologically, when relationships are fresh and when teachers are at their most enthusiastic. If a scheme starts just after a break then there is enough time for any initial obstacles to be overcome before the next break.

Most schools have everything ready and start the scheme operating directly after the initial meetings and only with parents who have come to the meetings. They then put into operation their special arrangements to contact other parents as soon as possible.

IMPLEMENTING THE SCHEME

One of the main factors in the success of a home-reading scheme is good communication between parents and teachers. Teachers need to ensure that they are easily available and easy to talk to, particularly near the start of a project. This is where the partnership principle must really work as teachers need the kind of feedback that only parents can give.

The comment sheet

The comment sheet can be a good means of communication, but for parents who cannot use it fully, opportunities for talk with teachers have to be made. We must remember that if we do invite parents' comments, we should not be offended by criticism. One parent wrote that certain Ladybird books were 'boring and repetitious' – perhaps this is fair comment!

Teachers do find that writing on the comment sheet is a time-consuming activity, but a necessary one to set up a good dialogue. It is not enough simply to write down the date and title of the book. The following are some extracts from comments exchanged between a teacher and parents in the infant school referred to in Chapter 8:

Teacher	Parent
	I'm not sure what you want Ruth to focus on at the moment and whether I'm 'doing things right' – the present series of books doesn't seem to be stretching her much.
I take your point. She doesn't read with a lot of expression at school, but that's probably because she is fairly shy in school. I am sure she is much more confident at home. Try this series of books. Their content is much more varied.	
Bangers and Mash 12 This is his own choice. As most of the others will be choosing, I thought the 'everyday readers' ought to have a day when they choose so as not to feel left out. But it will be my selection for them Monday–Thursday.	
Bangers and Mash 13 and 14	He was quite sad at getting to the end of these! I feel the last three or four have been a bit difficult, although his enjoyment of them has helped.
Trig 1. I offered him a free choice!	Read this through three times in about five minutes! He said it was a bit easy for him and he'd find something harder next time!
Trig 3 and 4. I tried to persuade him to change series but *no way*. So I've sent two at a time!	

Home visits

Home-visiting is obviously a very time-consuming activity and teachers can feel very hesitant about contacting parents at home for various reasons. Where parents do not find it easy to approach teachers in school and do not make written comments, this way of keeping in touch can be particularly important. Essentially it demonstrates the willingness of the school to meet parents on their own ground and shows that teachers do not always expect parents to come to them. On such visits, encouragement and appreciation need to be offered, as well as advice and guidance.

EVALUATING THE SCHEME

Ways of evaluating the scheme have been discussed earlier in the chapter. Whatever kind of evaluation is chosen, it is important that at some stage all parties review both their own contribution and the scheme as a whole. It is in the nature of a partnership like this that a considerable amount of time should elapse before attempting evaluation. This is not a concentrated or dramatic form of intervention but one which is gradual and long lasting, an extension, albeit a special one, of teaching and learning in school.

If a scheme has been launched near the beginning of the academic year, then it would be reasonable to reflect on it near the end of the first year.

The four main reasons for evaluating a home-reading project can be seen in the form of questions to be answered:

1 Have our aims for the project been realised?
2 Are there any other changes, ones that we did not envisage, to which we should respond?
3 Has the project been worth the effort expended? Do we want to continue?
4 What modifications or developments do we need now?

The research seems to indicate the following:

1 Aims have been discussed in the planning stage. Indicators of change may be specifically in reading achievement; or the school might also have wider aims to do with home/school relations.
2 Some schools have reported that once parents became more confident and more knowledgeable, they took more interest in other aspects of learning in school, or expressed anxieties that they had kept to themselves previously.

   Some teachers report that other aspects of children's well-being have emerged through the regular communication between parent and teacher.

   Schools sometimes feel that they need to reappraise their views on teaching reading as a result of working with parents on a home-reading scheme. As they have to make clear to parents and discuss how they see reading, they themselves may start to question their perceptions.

   Sometimes schools will want to look again at the reading material they are offering to children and the amount of choice they give.
3 This question depends on how far the school feels that their aims have been realised.

4 One development that could well come out of running a home-reading scheme is that the school would like to set up a school bookshop. This can be a very valuable extension of the scheme particularly when it can be run in partnership with parents.

Teachers might feel that now that children are reading more, they would like to make regular contact with the local library and the children's librarian.

Frequency of reading with parents has already been discussed – this might be altered as the scheme reaches its second phase. It might be a good idea to give the scheme a 'rest' in the second half of the summer term, for instance.

As children become more fluent readers, shared reading with parents might take the form of silent reading with discussion afterwards. Plans for talking to some parents about this may need to be made.

SUMMARY AND CONCLUSIONS

This chapter began with a brief case study of an infant school starting to implement a home-reading scheme. It continued by considering many of the factors present in planning, implementing and evaluating a scheme and how these factors might be accommodated in a typical infant school setting. The planning stage was considered at some length because it was felt that the quality and depth of the thinking and discussion at this stage has far-reaching implications for the success of a project. The other most important factor in a scheme like this was seen to be the regular two-way communication between parent and teacher.

4 A home-reading project in first schools

The use of case studies is a helpful way of making certain points. They are the adult, written equivalent to the child's anecdote. The reader or listener can more clearly appreciate the message because of the story form. Teachers can identify with the participants and the situations they find themselves in. A case study can also provide a focus for discussion and subsequent action.

This chapter is given over to a description of a home-reading project carried out simultaneously in six first schools in a Midlands town. While the project was, by and large, successful, the account shows how educational research can be anything but the tidy process it is sometimes made out to be – at least when it gets to the stage of being written for publication.

By describing the project in some detail it is hoped that readers might gain some insight into the kind of tasks that can confront a teacher turned temporary researcher. After all, many teachers in primary schools embark on diplomas, higher degrees or teacher fellowships that require some small-scale research, or they may be seconded by their LEA to gather and analyse various kinds of information. Other readers may be starting up projects of their own and this account might help them to avoid some of the pitfalls. The account of this project cannot be termed 'uplifting' or 'inspiring' but it is interesting in many respects. It reflects an ordinary working situation where change and innovation were sought without vast expenditure of time or resources.

HOW DO PROJECTS START?

In 1979 the results from the Haringey Reading Project were being disseminated. In a Midlands town, teachers were aware of the results to varying degrees. They were largely unmoved; almost all their schools sent books home, so what, they thought, was all the fuss about? Some of the teachers in six of the first schools in the town were, however, about to be involved in a home-reading scheme.

This state of mild interest must have been fairly typical of many schools not in inner-city areas at that time – perhaps even of some schools now. These schools all had their own priorities then, and involving parents in children's reading was not one of them. Yet it might be fair to think that many such projects were being set up in the wake of Haringey and Belfield.

The initiative for the project came from the LEA. Often schemes of this kind begin with one teacher in a school deciding to try out for herself what she has been reading and hearing about. Sometimes whole schools or departments decide by consensus that this is something they want to try; at other times the head or, as in this project, an adviser or inspector, is the prime mover.

It is not difficult to see that the way in which a project is started carries considerable implications for the enthusiasm and consistency with which the project is carried through and, ultimately, for its success. The ideal way to start something off is surely from unanimous enthusiasm within the school, coupled with interest and long-term support from without. Added to this should be a fairly clear idea of what is being aimed for and a way of assessing whether the aims have been fulfilled. If a reasonable amount of finance for new books is also forthcoming then the omens must be good.

In this particular case the 'status' of the project was quite high and it was being run on experimental lines, which usually gives schemes an initial boost. On the other hand, it did not arise out of the perceived needs of children and teachers within the schools. The project was taken on with varying degrees of enthusiasm and conviction by teachers and heads. Ultimately the varying degrees of satisfaction and success reflected, as you would expect, the degree of commitment of the teachers concerned. That is not to say that *all* the teachers were not vitally concerned with raising their children's achievement in reading, but rather that they did not necessarily see parents as partners in this work.

HOW THE READING PROJECT STARTED

The home-reading project was started as a direct spin-off from the Haringey Project described in Chapter 1. The idea of setting up and monitoring a home-reading scheme was put to the heads of the six selected schools in the summer term, prior to what was originally meant to be a year-long project. No detailed plans were laid at that time. In the September there was a planning meeting of heads; they had now secured the co-operation of the teachers who would be running the project. Again in September, a headteacher from Haringey and some of her staff came to talk to the heads and teachers concerned.

The model that was successful in Haringey was to be taken up, the basic ingredients being to:

1   make contact with parents and explain the project to them;
2   arrange for parents to listen to their child read aloud twice-weekly at home;
3   have some kind of a home/school reading record card to be the basic means of contact;
4   carry out some kind of standardised reading test before and after intervention.

The fifth basic ingredient present in the Haringey Project but absent in this project was the presence of the two researchers, J. Hewison and W. Schofield, who worked with individual parents in their own homes throughout the project. This difference would emerge as significant. In his final report of the Haringey Project to thc DES, W. Schofield set the scene for such a project as this:

> The research staff were a resource not normally available in schools. Thus an important outstanding question would seem to be how successful parent involvement might be if organised directly by the LEA through the head and class teachers without the intervention of any other persons visiting homes and inevitably fostering co-operative attitudes.

It was decided by the LEA to use Young's *Group Reading Test* in its parallel forms before and after the project. (This test includes word/picture-matching and sentence completion.) Unfortunately, the testing did not take place in all six schools until late October. (Half-term was imminent so nothing happened until early November.) After the half-term break, four schools' projects were under way. The other two schools were not able to start in the autumn term at all and did not in fact start until late January/early February. One result of the delay was that these children's reading test results were not included in the final analysis. Qualitative data, however, *was* collected from all the schools, through interviews with parents, children, heads and teachers, and this will be referred to later.

Exactly how each school started will be explained briefly later; it was agreed at the initial meeting that each school would run its own scheme in its own way within the four-point framework mentioned earlier.

BACKGROUND INFORMATION ON THE SCHOOLS AND THE CHILDREN

Four of the six first schools involved were on their own site and two were first school departments of combined schools. Five out of the six schools were grouped near to each other in the same part of the town – the less prosperous part. The housing was all 'respectable'. There was a large number of council houses, some Victorian terraced houses, and a new private housing estate. The vast majority of families in these schools could be called working-class. The sixth school had a more balanced mix of socio-economic groups.

Except for one school, each school had a large number (around 40%) of British Asian children, mostly born in the town, whose parents or grandparents had originally come from the Punjab. These families mainly had Punjabi as their mother tongue and were of the Sikh religion.

The unemployment rate amongst parents was around or slightly above the national average. In two of the schools there was a considerable number of children from single-parent families and also a number of children whose home life was not always easy.

The target age groups in each school were third and fourth-year classes – six, seven and eight year-olds. One larger school had two classes in each year group, and it was decided that one class in each year should act as a control, although, as it worked out, the control groups were not quite what they seemed – but more of this later. Before the start of the Project, children in four of the schools took their 'reader' home with them to encourage parents to listen to their child's reading. In two of the schools books were only sent home at the parents' request. In one of these two schools children were required to reach a reading age of around 5·5 before they were allowed to take their reader home. Three of the six schools allowed children to take books of their own choosing home on occasions.

THE STRUCTURE OF THE PROJECT

As referred to earlier in the chapter, there was agreement between the heads of the six schools as to how the project should be run, the model being that of the Haringey Project. The proposals were briefly as follows:

1   Schools were to introduce the project to parents and encourage their participation in the way that they thought best. No parents should be unduly pressured to join the project but it would obviously be good if

All teachers are actually concerned with children's reading.

they all did – both from the children's point of view and from the point of view of assessment.

2   The project would run for one school year and the decision as to whether it should be continued/modified/developed would be left to individual schools after that.

3   There would be a payment of £50 per class from the LEA for extra books that would be needed.

4   Teachers would arrange for children to take home books other than class readers on a rota basis twice or three times weekly. The books would be at an independent reading level.

5   A comment sheet for communication between parent and teacher would go with the book. There would also be printed guidelines to help parents.

6   The class teacher would monitor the reading done at home, how and when she felt necessary.

7   Young's *Group Reading Test* would be administered to the target groups of six and seven year olds before and after intervention. This would be one means of evaluating the project.

8   One third-year class group and one fourth-year group in the larger school would be used as control groups.

THE DURATION OF THE PROJECT

The delay in the administration of the Young's *Group Reading Test*, mentioned before, resulted in four schools starting after half-term in the autumn and two schools early in the next year. The post-intervention reading tests had to be carried out in June of the following year, because of the researchers' dissertation deadline. Gradually and for various reasons, the project running time was whittled down to six months instead of the full year. As anyone who has been concerned with home-reading schemes will know – and as shown repeatedly in the published accounts of projects – they probably need to run for at least two years for the full results and implications to become apparent. Six months can give indications and reveal certain factors, but it is not long enough for the delicate and complex forces in a home/school partnership to become fully operational.

ESTABLISHING CONTACT

All the schools set about contacting parents in slightly different ways and obtained different levels of support for different reasons. The schools will be referred to as Schools A–F. Three out of the six schools (A B and C) obtained base one hundred per cent support almost immediately, in varying ways. The head of school A had a relatively close relationship with all the families in the school. After the initial meeting in school, non-attending parents contacted the school and soon everyone was involved. School B (whose results were not included in the reading test analysis) had a good record of parent participation. After the initial meeting which followed a parents' assembly, the non-attending parents were sent an explanatory letter with a reply slip. In school C there was no initial meeting for parents; they were informed by letter that they were now expected to listen to their children read at home twice a week. School D's initial meeting of parents was not well attended so the head arranged individual interviews, involving more parents this way. School E had an initial meeting followed up by a special meeting for Asian mothers, with an interpreter. Many parents in this school were recruited to the scheme after it had started. Parents were asked to sign a 'contract' confirming that they would listen to their child read regularly. School F arranged two initial meetings but only managed to contact 50% of the families. At that time they had just embarked on a new science curriculum which involved some home-based research; this was their priority.

All in all, over the six schools, after the initial period, 65% of the children in the target classes had joined the project – 120 children in all. Thirty-nine children joined the project in the next few weeks. These were mostly children from Asian families who joined after individual contacts had been made with their parents. Forty-one children did not join the project because their parents chose not to participate. Fifty-five more children were included in the research – they represented the children in two control classes in a large first school. In total, 255 children were included in the investigation.

Frequency of reading to parents

It was originally proposed that parents would listen to their child read either twice or three times a week. When the schemes were run in the different schools, one school opted for once a week and another school decided on every weekday evening. Out of the remaining four schools, three schools went for twice-weekly and one school for three times. When it came to analysing the results of the reading test, the frequency with which books were taken home was used as a variable.

KEEPING IN TOUCH

In all schemes for involving parents in children's reading, one factor is vital if the partnership is to reach its full potential for the child, and that is good communication. This is true whether parents are collaborating at home or in school. There are many different ways of keeping in touch and it would seem that the more thought and time that can be put into this aspect of the scheme, the better.

The comment card

Out of the six schools, two schools (A and C) did not use a comment card. In school A it was felt that there was already enough opportunity for parents and teacher to talk together and a card was not needed. In school C, where there was no initial meeting with parents, the comment card was not discussed. In the other four schools this device was used in different ways; one school just had parents and teachers initial the cards, another used them for extended exchanges.

Meetings

Apart from the initial meetings, none of the schools held any other meetings.

Informal contacts

The teachers in the project took advantage of incidental meetings to ask about progress, and a few parents in the project took the initiative here. During open evenings held at the schools in the summer there was some discussion of the scheme. Some parents, both those who had joined the project and those who had not, did not come to school at all. These parents might well have been those who were not writing anything on the comment card either, so altogether there was very minimal contact with this group.

Home visits

As stated earlier in this chapter, teachers saw the absence of a researcher to liaise between home and school as a serious drawback in the design of the project.

Before turning to the results of this project, it is important to give a little more detailed explanation concerning aspects of the research design and implementation.

USING THE MODEL OF ANOTHER PROJECT

The joint meeting of teachers from Haringey and teachers from the project schools, together with information already circulated about the Haringey Project, had a definite effect on the expectations and attitudes of the local teachers.

Firstly, the local teachers perceived their project as being a copy of the Haringey Project and a poor imitation at that. Some schools throughout the year referred to the reading project as the 'Haringey Project', perhaps unconsciously implying that it was something borrowed rather than home-grown.

Secondly, the Haringey Project proper had enjoyed the help of the two researchers who had been in constant touch with parents at home. The local teachers throughout the project regarded this as a missing vital link for which they were not able to compensate. This recognition of a missing element might have stood in the way of schools strenuously working to find their own ways of maintaining good contact with parents.

Thirdly, the Haringey Project's remarkable results may have daunted the teachers. An obviously successful model is not always the best to emulate. The local teachers noted two factors from the Haringey Project which bore on their own. These were:

1   In one of the schools, the only reading scheme before the project was the Ladybird Key Word Scheme.
2   There was no previous practice of taking books home regularly.

From the local teachers' point of view it was no wonder that when these two factors were changed, dramatic improvements in reading followed. These two conditions did not obtain in local schools – teachers could foresee that the 'before and after' pictures would be vastly different from those in Haringey and were concerned about this.

USING A STANDARDISED READING TEST AS A MEASUREMENT OF SUCCESS

In this home-reading project the Young's *Group Reading Test* was used as an indication as to the success of the project. When such schemes are run on an experimental basis it is quite usual for schools or LEAs to use a standardised reading test. There are considerable drawbacks, however, inherent in this method of evaluation.

Looking at the test itself – it is in part a word recognition test and in part a discrete sentence completion test. Its advantage is that it is cheap and easy to administer. Its disadvantages are numerous and shared with many other reading tests:

1   The test does not reflect in any way the kind of reading material that children encounter in every other aspect of their lives.
2   The model of reading it typifies is in part a narrow hierarchical skills-based model (the word recognition) and in part a limited language-based model, seeing the *sentence* as the unit of meaning rather than discourse (the discrete sentence completion).

Compare these two narrow mechanistic aspects with the objectives the teachers had in mind for the reading project. They wanted the children to develop a more positive attitude towards all their reading which would perhaps be reflected in other areas of the curriculum as well. They wanted the children to develop a greater interest in reading and be willing to read more reflectively. They wanted to build up better contacts with parents. When you put these objectives against the skills measured in the reading test, the lack of alignment is obvious.

There *are* materials that give some measure of the movement in attitudes towards reading. For instance, in the experimental project in Coventry schools referred to in *Raising Standards* (Widlake and Macleod, 1984), the Hunter Grundin Literacy Profiles were used. As the authors of the book explain, these tests were recently standardised (1978–1982) and offer an imaginative and wide ranging approach. Of the five tests making up the profiles, one assesses attitude to reading, and another reading for meaning. The other three tests are concerned with spelling, free writing and spoken language.

3   If standardised tests *are* being used, they need to be up-to-date. The Bullock Report warns against using outdated tests, even if the norms have been up-dated, and recommends not using tests more than ten years old.

4   The whole dilemma of using a standardised reading test at all is summed up by Keith Gardner in *Testing Reading Ability*: 'A test provides the means by which a competence or lack of competence in *those abilities measured by the test* can be shown. Actual reading performance may be determined by factors other than competence to achieve under test conditions.'

Young's *Group Reading Test* is obviously popular; it was being used by 30 LEAs. To quote from Gipps and Wood (1981) it is '. . . simple to administer, quick and cheap, and teachers like it'. The idea, though, that children's progress in reading or any other aspect of learning follows a smooth upward gradient, is false. Understanding comes in fits and starts and there are many plateaux when efforts are consolidated and even times, especially with reading, when we want to retrace our steps.

5   Using reading tests sometimes makes teachers put aside their own valid subjective assessment of the situation. The teachers in the reading project, as testing time approached, would comment on what they saw as improved attitudes or a better grasp of reading, then add '. . . but of course, we'll have to see what the tests show'.

There are, of course, alternative methods of evaluation. A diary of comments on each child's reading, recording anything that seems significant as well as the books read, can be very useful. Entries could come from observations from parents and teacher, from talking about books as well as from listening to children read aloud. Children can record lists of books read in a simple 'log' with headings like:

Book title

Author

Did you finish the book?   Yes/No

Did you like it?   a lot/a bit/not at all

Date started

Date finished

Teacher's initials

Teachers can also note how often children choose reading when there is an opportunity for choice of activity; how they behave in the book corner; how children either settle quickly into their reading at the quiet reading times or are not easily absorbed. Many similar observations quickly jotted down can form patterns that give a fuller picture of the child as a reader than any reading test.

Amassing qualitative data is clearly a lengthier task than administering a test, but the process is valuable in itself. It is useful to have a record to reflect back on over a period of time and the data can be used for diagnostic purposes.

OBTAINING PARENTAL RESPONSE

A comment card or sheet of some kind is generally needed in this kind of scheme, but not all parents automatically respond to the opportunity for being in written communication with the teacher – they need encouragement and sometimes guidance. Parents who have been kept at arm's length previously or who are diffident about their role as partners are not readily going to start a fluent dialogue with the teacher – they are not sure if she really wishes to have one. Some parents may be unsure of what is expected of them under the heading 'Comments'; do teachers want a list of words that were not read correctly or something more general? Teachers need to be aware, too, that some parents do not have command of written English, either because they have another mother tongue or because they are concerned about their spelling and grammar.

It is certainly very difficult in a first or infant school for a teacher to be released for home visits, especially in smaller schools. The only possibilities are for either non-teaching heads to cover for the teacher, or for classes to 'double up' for a short time. In some schools, where there is a substantial number of children for whom English is not their mother tongue, extra teachers are employed under a special DES provision. They are commonly called 'Section Eleven' teachers. Part of their time might be taken to cover the project teacher's class, releasing the latter for home-visiting. In the final analysis it is a question of priorities – time can always be made for something that is considered really important.

There are wider implications attached to home-visiting apart from time and staffing. In some schools there is an assumption that teachers need to instruct parents, and obviously the best place to do this, from the teacher's point of view, is in school – on *their* home ground. As soon as the venue for talk changes, then necessarily the tone of the talk must change as well.

Primary school teachers are often teased that they talk to all adults as though they were five-year-olds in school. There can sometimes be truth in the taunt, though certainly the fault is not deliberate. In-service sessions using role play and the video can identify and remedy the problem.

The awkwardness that some teachers feel when exchanging views and information with parents, may be due to the lack of two elements:

1 the conviction that parents do really have a vital role to play and that a partnership is important;
2 confidence in oneself as a teacher and in one's own understanding of reading and language. Confidence should not produce closed minds but adequate confidence is a foundation for articulating views on both experience and current thinking.

LOOKING AT THE VARIABLES AND FINDINGS OF THE MIDLANDS PROJECT

There were many variables in this project which might have been considered when interpreting the pre- and post-intervention reading scores. There was, though, a limit to the time and opportunity for either the researcher or the teacher to gather information. Also, for various reasons, mostly concerned with a dissatisfaction with the reading test, it was decided to spend as much time as possible collecting and collating qualitative data – descriptive material by which to try to assess the success or otherwise of the project. The variables considered (with findings) were as follows:

Project status

There were four categories:

(a) in project;
(b) joined later;
(c) not in project;
(d) not included in project.

These categories refer to the 255 children included in the research:

(a) in project: 120 children who joined the project in its initial stages;
(b) joined later: 39 children who joined in the early weeks of the project;
(c) not in project: 41 children whose parents chose not to participate;
(d) not included in project: 55 children in two control classes.

The 'joined later' category was not used in the main part of the analysis of the reading test scores but was used to investigate whether non-English speaking mothers had been deterred from joining the project at its inception.

Findings
In all the following results an analysis of covariance was used. When the reading gain of the group of children who joined the project was compared with that of the group that did not join (the 'not in project' group), it was found that the group in the project had made significant gains over the group who had not joined (significance at the .01 level). When the project group was compared with the control group there was no difference. This was not really surprising as the teachers of the control classes were not in any way restricted as to their contact with parents over children's reading. It soon became evident that in those classes many children were reading to their parents more often than the children in the project!

Frequency of reading to parents

As mentioned previously, this varied between once a week and four times a week. This was an unlooked-for variation but advantage was taken of it to see if a higher frequency would produce better test score gains.

Findings
It was found, not surprisingly, that the more often children read with their parents, the better the reading gains tended to be.

Perseverance

This was a subjective assessment by the class teachers. They were guided by (a) responses on comment cards, (b) conversations with the children, and (c) regular monitorings of the reading done at home.

Findings
Perseverance certainly brought rewards – it was shown that where children and parents kept reading regularly, reading score gains were significantly higher than those of children whose parents had not been consistent.

English spoken by mother

It had been thought that when the mother did not speak or read English this might minimise the child's progress in the home-reading project.

Findings
As in the Haringey Reading Project, children whose mothers did not speak or read English were just as able to benefit from a home-reading scheme as children of English-speaking mothers. What did emerge though was that some non-English-speaking mothers may well have been reluctant to join

in the project and a high proportion of these mothers did not join the project initially, but joined later as the result of individual contacts.

Sex

In much of the literature about children's reading it is claimed that young girls attain higher reading scores in standardised tests.

Findings
It was found that girls did not score significantly higher than boys nor were their reading gains significantly greater than those of the boys.

Generally speaking, the children who joined the project showed more gains in the reading test conducted at the end of the scheduled six months of the project than those who did not. Within these results, though, there were many questions and uncertainties. For instance, why did some families not join and would those children have benefited in the same way if they had? This kind of research design and statistical analysis is probably well beyond the reach of most teachers. Nevertheless, all teachers can collect qualitative data, and it is to this that we turn next.

SUMMARY OF INTERVIEWS WITH PARENTS IN THE PROJECT

Fifteen families were interviewed at home, and these represented four out of the six schools. Thirteen of the families visited had joined the project, while two had not. Five of the interviews were with mothers only and ten were with both care-givers. Six of the families visited were British Asian. The purpose of the semi-structured interviews was to try to find out:

1   some general features of the home and family background;
2   how the reading was going on;
3   how parents saw the value of a home-reading scheme and how they felt about their role;
4   some pointers as to why the two non-participating families had not joined the project.

Families seemed genuinely pleased (and surprised) to be asked about their views and their side of the project. It was interesting to find out that none of the parents were aware that the same kind of project was being carried on in six first schools simultaneously. It seemed a pity that this opportunity of giving the project some added status had been missed. Many experimental projects obviously produce a Hawthorne effect – the very fact that they are being given attention tends to make the participants behave in a different (usually a more positive) way. On the other hand it is no bad thing, if all other aspects are favourable, to give a new venture an auspicious start, and as the novelty starts to wear off it is often helpful to have an interested outsider to monitor progress.

Family size

1 family had only 1 child
8 families had 2 children
4 families had 3 children
2 families had 4 children

The two families not in the project had 4 and 3 children respectively. This may well have been one of the reasons they did not join.

Parents' work patterns

Mother 5 mothers worked full-time
         5 mothers worked part-time
         5 mothers did not work outside the home

Father 5 fathers worked full-time
        1 father was unemployed
        9 fathers worked evening shift or late hours

In the two families which had not joined the project, both the mother and father worked full-time with both fathers working in the evening.

Socio-economic status (from father's occupation)

1   professional
2   self-employed (following redundancy)
1   clerical
11 manual or unemployed

Frequency of reading at home

3 children read five times in a fortnight
7 children read twice a week
3 children read once a week

Length of time spent reading to parent

6 children took approximately 15 minutes
6 children took 15–30 minutes
1 took a very varied amount of time

Who the child usually read to

2   children usually read to father
7   children usually read to mother
1   child often read to himself
3   children read on their own in their room

Does your child settle easily or have to be persuaded?

Eleven children were judged to settle readily and easily. Specific mention was made of one child who was much more willing now that he had more confidence. Two parents said that their children sometimes settled quickly and sometimes had to be persuaded. Some parents remarked that the summer evenings encouraged 'playing out' but on the other hand bedtimes tended to be later. Five parents judged their children to be 'hooked on TV'.

Whereabouts does your child read?

Most children read in the main living room which also contained the television set. One child read to her mother at bedtime in her bedroom.

Most children read in the main living room.

What kind of help do you give to your child?

The most common form of help was with difficult, unknown words. Help with awareness and regard to punctuation was mentioned several times. Encouragement to build more expression into the voice was also common. One child had help with word-building from his father, who taught him to isolate the stem of the word or to build up the syllables.

Many parents did express concern over children's monotonous reading and reading without recognising the sentence as a unit. This might well be a reflection of the way in which children read to the teacher in the classroom on occasions when the teacher's attention is divided between the reader and the many other members of the class.

Have you had/do you want any help and advice from school?

Three parents had obtained help and advice from their school, two through the comment sheets, one verbally. Eight parents had not obtained, nor did they look for, advice from school. One mother, while not seeking advice about reading for her own child, thought perhaps Asian parents might benefit from this and thought the project might provide a way for Asian children to help their mothers with English. One Asian mother was sure she did not want help from school. She saw her role as helping her child in a different way from teachers. 'We each have our own jobs to do.' (There were in fact guidelines written on the comment sheet but no parent referred to these.)

Use of the comment sheet

About half the parents commented on the sheets – the other half only wrote their initials. (At the final meetings of heads and teachers examples were shown of project sheets which were providing feedback in both directions for parents and teachers. The difficulties of Asian parents who did not write in English were discussed.) One father suggested that many parents might be diffident or unsure what kind of comment was considered appropriate. Another parent remarked that it seemed as though the comment column was for teachers only.

Has the project been easy to keep up?

Most parents agreed that it had been reasonably easy. Many parents observed that 'once you get into the habit, it is easier.'

Did you listen to your child read before you joined the project?

Previous practice varied from the case of a parent whose child had transferred from a school where reading books were not taken home, to one in which parents had listened to their child read most evenings before the project started and were now doing less.

Do you think that, on the whole, the books brought home are suitable?

About half the parents remarked that they thought the books were mostly too simple (the implication here was that parents were unsure of their role if it was not to be instructional). One mother expressed exasperation with Janet and John and couldn't understand how any child could enjoy reading it; she remembered hating it when she was at school! The parents of one child still struggling through the supplementary books of another scheme commented similarly. One father remarked about his son, a failing reader, 'I think it's [Kathy and Mark] repetitive and boring, but I don't see how reading at this stage can be otherwise – I don't think John is bored'.

Two parents commented that the reading level at the beginning of the project seemed too high and the passages took too long to read aloud, but felt that towards the end the books were getting much easier and 'a bit of a waste of time'. One parent stated that her son often read the book on the way home from school. Another parent contrasted the relatively easy level of the book sent home with her child's voluntary reading habits which included *The Secret Seven* by Enid Blyton.

One mother expressed concern over the problem of continuation of a story over two project nights. She always had to revise the beginning of the story, and felt that interest was lost. One interesting comment from the mother of a competent reader was that because of the project he was no longer allowed to bring home his reading scheme books and was now unable to complete the scheme before transfer to the middle school. This had caused the child considerable disappointment!

Why did you decide to join the project?
Do you think it's right to ask parents to help like this?

Most responses were similar and general: 'I thought it would be good for him/her.' The parents of the less competent readers were aware that their children were struggling and appreciated a structured schedule for reading at home. The parents of one school were not aware that they had a choice over joining. One family was on the point of looking for private tuition prior to the project. One mother remarked 'They're my children. I've got to do my bit as well.' Another commented: 'I think it's a parent's job to help all they can.' Two Asian parents expressed satisfaction that the children were being asked to do things at home. They felt that the children watched too much TV and played too much.

Parents seemed to be aware of economic pressures affecting education, especially in the first schools, and this may have affected their willingness to help. Only one father thought that it was the job of the school to provide all the help needed for reading (he was, however, an extremely consistent participant in the project).

What do you think your child has got out of the project?
Is he/she reading more now?

Largely, responses fell into two categories. Firstly, parents of less competent readers felt that their children had gained a lot of confidence and felt there was also an improvement in their reading. One father noticed that his child was reading road signs and asking about words on public notices. Secondly the competent readers were thought by their parents to have gained more fluency and seemed to be getting more meaning from the text. These children were already committed readers. One mother's comment that expressed a very important aspect of the project was: 'It's brought her closer to me – she'd always been a Daddy's girl.'

Parents' own reading

In only two homes were there books in evidence. Reference was made in some homes to the children's books in their bedroom. Of course there may also have been books in other rooms as well. In six homes a daily paper was delivered and one further home had a regular periodical. In five particular instances it was clear that the mother enjoyed reading. In one instance the father enjoyed reading and in two cases they both spent time reading. There was one instance of the whole family 'hooked on books'.

Parents' schooling

The majority of the parents interviewed had left school at the statutory leaving age (fifteen in their cases). Two Asian mothers left school at thirteen which, apparently, was customary. Five parents expressed the recollection that they were 'glad to go'.

Parents spoke of their feeling that in the secondary school, teachers were only interested in you if you were bright. They contrasted the warm memories they had of primary school with those of secondary school.

Using the public library

For the child this depended to a large extent on locality. As the children were eight at the time of the project, if they did not live within safe walking distance of a library they were dependent on parents to take them. One father did not go or take the family to the library because they did not have enough science fiction books. One father whose son was struggling to read held out the promise of joining the library to his son 'when he could really read'. Eight children were regular borrowers at either the main library or a branch. Two mothers commented that they had stopped borrowing books because they did not return them on time.

Language spoken at home

Six Asian families were visited, five of which took part in the project. All the families except one spoke mainly Punjabi at home. In this one family the mother's first language was Hindi, but she spoke some English. The father had learnt some Hindi since their marriage and also spoke good English. His first language was Punjabi. The two children spoke mainly English and apparently replied in English when their father spoke to them in Punjabi! In all the Asian families visited, the task of helping the children with reading seemed to be informally shared between both parents. All the parents in those families seemed anxious that the children should learn to read and write well in Punjabi. Two families sent their children to evening school, two families had regular sessions at home, and the other two families had firm plans for this. One father put forward the view that 'being able to get your tongue around Punjabi was an excellent training for many languages'.

The 'openness' of school

How parents perceived this aspect of school was perhaps best reflected in their obvious general approval of their child's school and the feeling that they could readily consult teachers or the head if and when they needed to. The parents at one school did feel that the annual occasion set aside for talking with teachers was not enough. None of the parents was currently involved in helping in school. All the parents made an effort to attend all open evenings and some parents emphasised that they went to school whenever 'anything was going on'. Two parents spontaneously expressed interest in learning more about teaching methods. The researcher did not get the feeling that parents wanted more involvement with school at this point. This may have been partly because of working patterns. Also many Asian parents were themselves educated in a very formal way with a firm dividing line between home and school. Other parents had also not been accustomed to parental involvement when they themselves were children.

It was seen from the interviews with heads and teachers that they, too, felt that there was sufficient *involvement* of parents in schools, though they would like to develop better *contacts*.

Would you carry on with the project?

All the parents replied in the affirmative. Seven parents would welcome more extensive work from school. Three of these parents questioned the value of continuing reading aloud, but would like their child to have regular tasks set from school. Four of the Asian parents seemed really anxious that children should have some task set every day; they themselves often gave them sums to do. This anxiety that the children should 'work' rather than 'play' is commonly observed by teachers who often feel uneasy about this somewhat misdirected goodwill. If there had been good contacts built up between teachers and Asian parents through the reading project, perhaps mutual understanding of this problem could have emerged.

Reasons for not joining the project

It is obviously difficult to establish why particular families or groups of families did not participate. Both the families interviewed came from the school who had not followed up individual parents after the introductory meeting. They were both large families and the fathers were heavily engaged in the evenings. Both mothers did not speak English very well and this was found to be a factor affecting whether or not they came forward to join the project. In no way did the families seem unconcerned about their children's education. Both parents said they would join the project next year if they were asked again.

SUMMARY OF INTERVIEWS WITH CHILDREN IN THE PROJECT

Semi-structured interviews with children in the project were conducted in two schools. The children were interviewed in pairs and one threesome. It seemed a good idea to talk to groups of children who are friends rather than to individuls since it is less intimidating.

Many of the questions were concerned with how the project was being implemented at home and the children's responses coincided largely with the parents'. All the children interviewed seemed to approve of the project and affirmed that they were not 'fed up' with it. Children whose parents worked full-time were sensitive to their parent's tiredness at the end of a long day. As one Asian eight year-old girl put it: 'First I let her eat something and drink something, then I read to her.' There were many references to Dad being 'glued' to the television and generally it seemed to be the mother who was seen to be interested in books.

Asked about what kind of help their parents gave them, it was mostly help with difficult words. Parents did not seem to praise often. As one girl said: 'She sometimes says good, she sometimes doesn't; if she's had a weary day she doesn't say anything.'

When the children were asked how they felt about reading aloud, the more fluent readers stated that they preferred to 'read in their heads' because they could 'find out what was happening better'. Some of the children commented that it was more peaceful reading at home than at school.

Many children mentioned reading in bed and many said that if they hadn't got anything else to do they liked to read. When asked about the importance of reading there was a unanimous response that it was very important. The children found it difficult to express why this was so. One response was that 'you need to get to know words – words help you a lot'. Another response was that you need to read for your job – for reading letters and for paying bills.

When asked if they would be willing to continue, all the children answered in the affirmative. The more fluent readers intimated that they would rather do other tasks on a regular basis.

SUMMARY OF INTERVIEWS WITH HEADS

(Interviews took place before the final reading tests.)

Have you come across any major difficulties in the project?

No schools had any major difficulty in organising or implementing the project. The fears about books being lost seem to have been unfounded (in the course of the project, two children only were suspended from the project due to persistent non-return of books).

What do you expect to come out of the project?

Generally the heads of the six schools did not expect significant reading gains because (a) they already had an informal system of reading books at home, and (b) the reading standards were for the most part adequate to good. School B expected some improvement in the average to below average reader and the head of school C saw the regularising of practice as being beneficial to a few 'borderline' parents, giving them an incentive to take more interest in education. The head of school D saw their inability to contact non-participating parents and support doubtful parents as minimising any beneficial effects.

What do you hope for from the project, apart from any gains in reading?

This question was put in order to give heads an opportunity to express a desire for better contact with parents. (If no mention was made of this aspect, it was followed with a question to establish the degree of parent participation in school.)

The heads of school D and school E specifically mentioned better contacts with parents as being a hoped-for outcome from the project. The head of school E looked further – towards more social and cultural integration between indigenous and Asian parents. The heads of all six schools felt that parents had free access to school. School F had a nursery department and the head stated that good contacts were made and developed from there. Parents were involved in school activities to a certain degree in all of the schools, though some schools had no Asian parents involved at the present. No school used parents regularly for help in reading or literacy-based activities. No school had a parents' room. School E seemed to provide a good deal of social support and advice and it was in this school that teachers were perhaps least inclined to see parents as an educative resource.

Additional comments

In the final meeting of heads (before the results of the reading test were analysed) it was agreed that all schools would carry on next year with the reading project. Arrangement were put in hand for a co-ordinating meeting of all six schools early in the autumn. During the project, schools had not met on a formal basis, though the present author had to some extent been a source of information. There was general acknowledgment that Asian parents were not all able to carry on a written dialogue via the comment cards, and that priority should be given in the next year to making contact with these parents, either at home or in groups with an interpreter if necessary. General disappointment was again expressed at the lack of additional research staff to contact parents at home, to support, advise and provide feedback for schools. As has been mentioned before, this need was keenly felt and continually expressed by heads and teachers. It may well be that if at the beginning of the project there had been an effort to make a virtue out of using only the resources of the school, this latent feeling of resentment may have been avoided. Schools could then have found their own ways of reaching parents.

SUMMARY OF INTERVIEWS WITH TEACHERS IN PROJECT SCHOOLS

This summary is based on semi-structured interviews with teachers in groups in individual schools, nearing the end of the project, before the reading test results were available.

Who chooses the books to go home – on what basis are they chosen?

In the main, the class teacher chose the book to be taken home, the book usually being at the independent level. Supplementary readers or books at a colour code level one below current reader were usually chosen. Some older, more fluent readers selected their own books which were generally longer. This group experienced some discontinuity as in most cases 'project books' were reserved for 'project' evenings and not read at other times. In one school two children regularly helped in the organisation but in all the other schools the teachers administered selection themselves, taking on average about 30 minutes. One teacher expressed doubt as to whether this time was being profitably spent, and wondered if it might not have been better spent in helping individual children with reading difficulties.

What was the level of parental response – either via the comment card or verbally?

Two schools, as previously mentioned, did not use comment cards. Out of the remaining four schools only one teacher seemed to have maintained a consistent level of communication through the comment card, using it for extended advice and comments. For the rest there seemed only a minority of cases where the card provided a meaningful contact. None of the schools had planned for verbal feedback and in none of the schools did teachers visit homes. Informal feedback was sometimes obtained when opportunities presented themselves and one school had obtained many favourable comments on parents' evening just prior to the end of the project meeting.

How well are parents persevering with the project?

The response to this question had to be based on the initialling of the comment cards and informed questions to children. All schools had the impression that most parents who had joined the project were being consistent, the exception being a small minority seen by schools as being difficult to motivate.

Do you think parents need more help and guidance?

Four out of six schools had sent home or given out written guidelines at the introductory meetings. Advice had also been given at the meetings. Individual help had occasionally been given. Due to lack of feedback, teachers could not be sure as to whether parents would have appreciated further help or advice. Some teachers did speculate that Asian mothers may well have needed help and encouragement. Many instances had been reported of fathers and older siblings helping the child where mothers could not read English.

Can you see any evidence of improvement in children's reading and attitudes to reading and school in general?

Many teachers referred at this point to their previous practices of encouraging reading at home. They all agreed that the children were still enthusiastic about the project and reminded teachers if they forgot. There was some mention of improved attitude and reading performance in some individual cases. One teacher felt that the children in the project were more reflective in their reading and more self-reliant in their approach to written instructions. Many teachers felt that the period of close contact with a parent where the child received undivided attention was likely to be the most beneficial aspect. Most teachers wanted to suspend judgement until results of the reading test were available. Teachers in two schools thought that in any case many fourth-year children 'made a spurt' with reading and doubted if any real gain could be associated with the project. One teacher felt that a period of SRA work had been more beneficial than the project.

Has it been worthwhile – will you carry on with the project next year?

All the six schools had decided to continue the project – heads and teachers being in agreement. The school with the 'control' groups had decided to extend the project to all the third and fourth-year classes. All teachers agreed that the children had appreciated the new books which had been bought for the project. The question of home-visiting had not been resolved.

SUMMARY AND CONCLUSIONS

This chapter has described an experimental home-reading project that was carried out in six first schools. It has recounted and analysed the many and complex processes within a project of this kind, from its inception, through its organisation, implementation, and finally to its evaluation. It has tried to show not only the successes, perhaps not even primarily the successes gained, but rather the underlying feelings and dynamics of the venture. Lastly, it shows the difficulties of evaluating projects such as this in a way which satisfies the participants. Indeed the true benefits from this kind of collaboration between parents and teachers must come only after a considerable period of time and will be so bound up with changes in behaviour from all three parties concerned that it will be almost impossible to identify a causal relationship.

5 A home-reading/learning scheme in a multicultural middle school

The previous chapter described how six first schools implemented an experimental home-reading scheme. This chapter deals with children from two of those schools who had moved on to a middle school. The present author, who monitored the project whilst on a year's secondment, had returned to this same middle school. It was decided that an attempt should be made to continue and develop the collaboration already present.

BACKGROUND TO THE SCHEME

This is an account of a year's home-reading/learning scheme which took place in a middle school for eight to twelve year-olds. The scheme involved all the sixty-five first year children, who were taught in two class groups. Most of the children had taken part in a pilot home-reading project in their first schools immediately before coming to the middle school. The school wanted to capitalise on the goodwill and interest that had been generated.

The pattern of the home-reading scheme in the first school had been that of reading aloud to parents twice a week. Communication between parents and teachers had been effected through the means of a comment sheet as well as some meetings and written guidelines produced by the school. One school had been more committed to the scheme than the others, and had taken more time and trouble over communicating with parents. Nevertheless, all parents had been willing to join in, albeit with varying degrees of perseverance.

A sizeable minority of the children coming to the middle school still experienced some difficulty with their reading; the majority did not. From the previous research (see Chapter 4) it was evident that both parents and children had grown somewhat impatient with reading aloud when the children were fluent readers. In fact, some children had tacitly abandoned this practice, and were just reading silently for a set time at home, with parents signing the comment sheet to the effect that the child had read.

AIMS OF THE SCHEME

The aim was to build on and to develop further and more widely the reading that had been established in the first schools. Not only did the school want children to read and enjoy books that they had chosen, but it also wished to involve parents in helping children read for information and in other areas of language development.

Like many other schools that have been involved in collaboration with parents, the school looked not only for gains in reading, but for other benefits to the children, parents and to the school. It was felt that these should include more positive attitudes towards reading, borne out by more voluntary reading. It was hoped that the children who were still experiencing difficulty with their reading would be helped to become more interested in reading and be able to better use their reading for learning purposes.

Apart from gains in reading, the school was hoping for a change in parents' attitudes. At the time there was a degree of tension between some parents and the school, at the least an incomplete understanding and, with a few parents, antagonism. If the underlying home/school conflict of loyalties which some children must be experiencing could be alleviated, then children would be 'freer' to develop more positive attitudes towards their work in school. It was felt that by developing good relationships between parents and teacher in a way that was clear for children to see, and by organising learning experience that spanned home and school, some progress would be made towards reducing any conflict. Some mothers in the Asian families felt very diffident about coming into school. It was hoped that, through the scheme, closer links could be built up with these mothers. Signs that attitudes were changing and links were becoming stronger might include higher attendance of parents at school meetings and functions. In a few cases where children did not have a good record of school attendance, less absenteeism might be seen to be a positive sign.

THE CHILDREN'S HOME BACKGROUND

The children came almost entirely from working-class backgrounds. The school was situated in a council housing estate with some streets of older privately-owned terraced houses. At this time about 40% of the children were of Asian origin (mostly born in Britain of parents who originated in the Punjab), were mainly Sikhs and had Punjabi as their mother tongue. Some of the other children came from single-parent families where, in some instances, the adult relationships were continually changing.

ORGANISATION OF THE SCHEME

The scheme was prepared and run by the languge consultant in the school, who also spent about 75% of her teaching time with the children and teachers of the first year classes. As the scheme was experimental, this was probably a good way to start. Ordinarily, schemes of this nature are probably best organised by class teachers within a whole-school policy. There was, however, close collaboration with the two class teachers, who were favourably disposed towards the idea, but quite naturally unsure of the likely returns set against the time and effort required (a calculation that, surely, all teachers must attempt to do – whatever the activity or circumstance).

FREQUENCY OF HOME-READING/LEARNING

It was decided that a twice-weekly pattern would be the best. This was not always strictly maintained, and when the summer term came it was decided with all parties concerned that once-weekly activities were sufficient. The second half of the summer term was left 'fallow'. On lighter evenings many children wanted to be outside and it seemed wise to follow this natural 'rhythm' of the year.

MATERIALS

As the scheme was experimental, it was decided to try out a variety of materials and activities – to see which seemed to be the most suitable and which were liked by both parents and children, trying always to get parents involved in an active way. Sometimes the activities were matched to

It was decided to try out a variety of materials and activities . . . trying always to get parents involved in an active way.

Often the tape was listened to by younger brothers and sisters.

individual children and at other times groups or whole classes took the same activities home. The activities were as follows:

1 A few children kept the practice of reading to and with a parent or older family member for much of the first term. Other, more fluent, readers sometimes read to themselves and, where possible, discussed or recounted their reading.

2 All the children who had a cassette tape-recorder at home took home a tape and book/s pack from the school's listening and reading resources. Children with reading difficulties had priority for borrowing these. Often the tape was listened to by younger brothers and sisters. This practice led to some children also taking books home and reading to them – a particularly valuable activity for those children with a poor image of themselves as readers.

3 Other reading activities were included from the Ginn 360 scheme, a language development programme for primary years. These were reading, summarising, reviewing and completing cloze texts. On reflection, this was not a suitable activity, partly because of the limited relevance of language exercises of any kind, and partly because the whole structure is too much like homework and precludes any real parental involvement, but rather puts parents in a purely supervisory role.

4 To improve spelling, short lists of words, either based on individual needs or words currently being used in an area of the curriculum, in this

Figure 5.1   Try it Again Spelling Sheet

WORD	TRY IT HERE	TRY IT AGAIN	LAST TRY

case Science, were taken home on the 'Try it Again' Spelling Sheet, ready-folded. (See Figure 5.1.)

The children had already been using the sheet in school and a letter was sent home to parents explaining to them how the sheet should be used and the basis for selecting the words. The main emphasis here was on *not* copying out the word but writing from memory. While in school, the children copied down the words in the *Word* column. (Here it was necessary to ensure that everyone had done this correctly as otherwise they would learn a misspelling, which would be hard to correct.) They were then reminded of the words and the contexts in which they were used.

The routine for using the sheets was as follows:

(a) Look carefully at the first word and say it aloud.

(b) Close your eyes and try to 'see' the word (or write it with your finger on the table top).

(c) *Turn over* the sheet so that you cannot see the word and write it from memory in the *'Try It here'* column.

(d) Turn back and check the spelling very carefully.

(e) If it is *right,* tick it and go on to repeat the same process with the next word.

(f) If it is *wrong,* turn back and look at the word again. Start the process again on this word – writing it out in the *'Try it again'* column.

The children were currently using the 'Try it Again' sheets in the classroom. After the initial experience they hardly ever 'cheated' by copying the word. Uncertain spellers were able to use this simple strategy to help them, and this, together with playing down their anxiety about their spelling, helped them not to go for the easy option.

Parents were asked to go through the sheets with their children. The response from parents was quite positive. They were interested to know something about learning spelling and could also clearly see the usefulness of this activity.

Parents were also made aware of what the children were doing in their Science-based topic about water and would sometimes ask questions about this.

5   Lastly, some Home-Reading/Learning packs were used. The packs are based around themes that span home and school and encourage children to develop and use their research skills. These packs originated from the Community Education Project in Coventry. The school later developed one pack of its own based on its neighbourhood. Initially, a pack about food was used (see Appendix). This went home and was used for two weeks. The work done at home was followed up and developed further in school as part of planned thematic teaching. Before the children took the pack home, the teacher explained its use, and parents were kept informed by letter. As home visits were under way by this time, many parents had had a preview of this pack.

The underlying rationale for this kind of learning activity is to directly involve parents in working with their child, in understanding the purposes of each different activity and in providing valuable feedback to the teacher. A vital part of the pack includes the introductory notes, the explanation of the skills that are being practised within each task and the concluding sheet which asks for general comments and a remark about each activity. Throughout the pack children are required to collect and collate information and then use it.

This model of working is removed from the traditional idea of homework in its involvement of the family and the choice of themes that use children's home experiences for their learning in school. When the work had been developed in school, a prominent display was mounted with a commentary about the whole project.

There was a deliberate decision to present a variety of tasks and activities to be worked on at home. This was because of the experimental nature of the project. When collaborating with parents in the normal context of the junior/middle school, it might be clearer to parents and children to have two different emphases and move from one to the other. The emphasis in one term might be on 'Reading more' and in another term on 'Reading for information'. A suggested brief outline for activities within these areas is offered in Figure 5.2.

VISITING HOMES

As an important part of the scheme, it was decided that there would be regular home visits. The decision was taken for the reasons shown on p.74.

Figure 5.2

A SUGGESTED YEAR PLAN FOR
INVOLVING PARENTS IN CHILDREN'S READING/LEARNING
IN THE JUNIOR SCHOOL

AUTUMN TERM – **Reading more Books**

Children read twice-weekly at home.
Parents could help by: reading the book themselves (sometimes) and
talking to child about plot, characters – child's and parent's response.

Book should be chosen by child and could be fiction or non-fiction.

A combined reading log/comment sheet could be used by
parents/children/teachers:

Date	Title	Author	Finished/ Not	Liked? a bit yes very much	Parent/Teacher's Comment

Supporting activities involving parents

Reviews and brief comments on books – to compile with parents and
children a current book of 'good books' to read (fiction and non-fiction).

To make links with books and plays currently on TV for children – to ask
for parents' co-operation and interest in this.

To have a book sale organised with local bookshop (fiction and
non-fiction).

For teachers, parents and children to compile a best books (fiction and
non-fiction) list to refer to on library visits or when buying books. This to
be updated regularly.

To compile a small library of books/tapes to be taken home – funds from
PTA. Parents invited to help as readers.

To involve parents in a Book Week.

In school

For parents to share books with small groups to discuss – recommend titles
– read and present extracts.

For children with reading difficulties

Aim . . . to read more – to see the benefits of reading.
Parents to share books at home based on children's choice and interests
(fiction or non-fiction).

These children to have priority with books/tapes.

Comment sheets between parents and teachers.
Regular contacts between parents and teachers.

FEEDBACK AND EVALUATION

Figure 5.2 continued

SPRING TERM

Extending reading, research and study skills

Developing, questioning and note-making based on home/school, reading/learning tasks.

Use of non-book material, e.g. maps, local papers, TV Times.

School could develop their own investigation sheets for using between home and school to either initiate or develop further the classroom work.

In school

Parents could join small groups to work on sheets – to discuss and talk about environment, neighbourhood, town, etc.

FEEDBACK AND EVALUATION

SUMMER TERM

LEAVE BLANK READY FOR NEXT TERM

1 It was an important way of making the scheme more effective – being able to explain the scheme and the materials, ask and answer questions, and to generally demonstrate the value of the scheme.

2 In the survey of six first schools who had initiated home/school reading projects, parents and teachers had said such contacts would be very beneficial.

3 One of the aims of the scheme was to establish better contacts between home and school. Visiting people's homes implies a willingness on the teacher's part to go more than half way to this end. It is a gesture which says more than the many verbal and written exhortations to parents to come into school.

Almost all the children's parents were visited at home over the course of a year. To cover for home-visiting teachers, the head took over the visiting teacher's commitment for one afternoon a week. Sometimes an evening visit was required, though this did not happen very often.

At the beginning of the project, a general communication included the information that home visits to all parents were planned, with parents' agreement. The purpose of the visits would be to discuss progress, reactions and difficulties relating to the scheme. In spite of this, and a short note just prior to the visit, many parents were anxious at the outset of the meeting. It had become the accepted norm that teachers did not go and see parents at home unless something serious had happened in school. When reassurance on this score was offered, the meetings were usually very friendly. Sometimes return visits were made when something needed following up, or where the initial contact seemed fragile and needed strengthening.

A diary of home visits was kept, recording any information that would lead to the modification or development of any of the scheme activities. It helped to monitor parents' reactions and also kept a record of points that needed follow-up in school.

Entries in the diary looked like this:

4 March	Mrs Rayner (Chris) – saw the little ones – lovely but lively! Mrs R. approves of the reading and working at home and says Chris likes it usually. He is v. keen on drawing at home – spends a lot of time on this. Explained and showed food pack to her.
	She is worried about Christopher's behaviour at school, from what she hears and from past experience. Persuaded her to come to open evening in a fortnight. Chat about bringing up families – a good visit.
2 February	Mr Kang (Inderpal). Inderpal away from school – visited anyway. Father v. worried about his reserve and slow progress – says he will be in the 'D' stream at secondary school. Explained response sheet again so that it is clear. Inderpal has completed the activity. Rarely reads except on this scheme so talked about taking him to the library. Inderpal v. lively at home but feels 'shy' of teachers. Mother was at school in England but father came here at 18 so no formal education in English. Punjabi spoken most of the time at home. Met uncle who had been to our school as a child years ago!
9 February	Mrs Matthews (grandmother of Andrew and Katy) – 2nd visit (see other book). Went to thank her for all she has done. Since taking home tape and story wallets they have started to buy a series of these. Saw Joanne (have seen her at first school). She liked the books Andrew brought home for her.
	Went through food pack – OK.
	Mrs M. has bought them some encyclopaedias.
	Obviously finds Katy a handful – told her she seems to be settling better in school.
	Katy was telling horrific stories about swimming sessions so they stopped them – put her right on this.

Most parents appreciated the home contact. Many of the parents visited did already come to termly open evenings, but some hardly ever came to school. The two-way nature of the visit was emphasised. It was not only to explain and encourage, but also to get genuine feedback on the scheme. The 'partnership' factor in such a scheme should become evident; it is surely easier to convey this when sharing a cup of tea in someone's home than when parents are sitting uncomfortably on a small chair in the classroom.

Much was learnt from these meetings. A much better understanding was gained of individual children when seen in their home background with their family. In particular, valuable learning came from visiting Asian families. Parents' concern was evident for their children's long-term prospects through education. There were many discussions about the balance that families were trying to maintain between the tensions of 'old' and 'new' ways of family and social life. Many of the young mothers felt isolated as they were not comfortable going out alone.

All the information, queries and discussions were useful, both in terms of learning more about the children's home background and, more subtly, for seeing them in a different situation. Relationships with the children deepened. Often children would want to discuss the visit again in school and were obviously pleased that the contact had been made.

Many teachers are very wary of visiting homes and some see such an activity as no part of their role as teacher. In all the projects that have received publicity in this area, teachers or their representatives have gone to the parents at home. The value of this activity is high, although it sometimes requires careful and sensitive handling. The main objective of the visits was to discuss the progress of the scheme by talking about and explaining materials, by answering queries and, most of all, by offering encouragement and support. In the course of the visits, many other topics arose concerning the child in question and also other members of the family, apart from queries and worries about school. This was a valuable aspect of the visiting.

COMMUNICATION

Good, regular communication is essential in all schemes involving parents. This was one of the factors brought out in Barry Stierer's recent report, following a project from the London Institute of Education, entitled 'Parental Help with Reading in Schools' (1985). His report looked at the role of reading helpers in schools and the implications of the practice of parental involvement in schools. Apart from home visits, regular communication was maintained through comment leaflets. These were the agent for a mutual exchange – on the teachers' part mostly requests and comments, on the parents' part feedback, queries, or just initials. Some parents used their leaflet extensively, some hardly at all. Discussion and promotion went on during home meetings, but always bearing in mind that some parents were barely literate, and many Asian parents did not write in English. Nevertheless, this kind of written communication can provide a record to which all three participants – teacher, parent and child – can refer. The front cover of the leaflet included a logo devised by the head, showing the close association of parent, teacher and child; this logo also went on the front cover of a school-produced work pack.

Communication also included meeting parents at school. There was a well-attended initial meeting outlining the scheme, preceded by an introductory circular. Parents talked about the scheme when they attended the open evenings; support and encouragement were offered. Some letters were sent out specifically to inform parents when new materials were about to be introduced.

Most of all, parents need encouragement and appreciation. All parents are concerned for their own children – indeed this is the dynamism on which such a scheme is built – but many parents are hard-pressed. Some of the parents in the scheme were on shift work, some were unemployed, some were the only care-giver. It needs to be conveyed to parents that their time, help and interest constitute a unique contribution to their child's learning, rather than an 'optional extra' to work in school.

ASIAN PARENTS AND CHILDREN

Quite a few of the Asian mothers did not read or write in English (this was not the case with fathers). A few mothers did not speak much English either. As such parents were diffident about coming into school, a home visit was all the more important.

As meetings at home were always by prior written arrangement, if necessary a more fluent English-speaking friend or relation would join in. A productive three-way exchange would then take place in English and Punjabi.

The spoken language patterns in these homes were interesting and varied from family to family. Mostly the children would talk to each other in English. Father and mother would converse in Punjabi, as would mother and children. Father and children would use a balance of Punjabi and English. All in all, for the children there was a truly bilingual environment. It seemed that all the parents wanted and took opportunities for their children to learn to read and write in Punjabi. From home meetings, the parents' high and serious expectations for their children were impressive. Almost always some form of higher or further education was envisaged, even at this early stage of schooling.

It was felt in school that most Asian parents (fathers in particular) had a fairly formal and sometimes rather narrow view of learning; there were numerous requests for homework in the form of repetitious exercises in computation and English comprehension. The regular, structured – but much wider – tasks of the home-reading/learning scheme helped to satisfy the demand for more work. This, together with discussion, was starting to move these parents away from their sometimes rather rigid concept of what constitutes a learning activity.

Filling in the comment leaflet was obviously a difficulty for some parents, though not all. Fathers were often involved. Many mothers often just gave their initials. Sometimes comments were written by children, dictated by their mother. The enthusiasm for the scheme was very high amongst Asian families in general.

EVALUATION

The discussion in Chapter 4 of the home-reading project in six first schools mentioned the use of standardised reading tests administered before and after intervention as a usual way of evaluating, wholly or partly, the success of such schemes. There are many problems with this method, some of which have been referred to earlier. One significant problem is the nature of the test itself: what exactly is being tested? The kinds of processes and changes that teachers hope must be taking place are not always amenable to quantitative testing.

Looking back to the aims for the scheme:

1   that children would develop greater interest and enthusiasm for reading all kinds of texts for different purposes;
2   that the few children having difficulty with reading would be helped by this scheme;
3   that there would be closer contact with home and that this would bring about more positive attitudes in parents towards school.

To see whether these aims were fulfilled we can examine the results of the scheme.

Interest and enthusiasm for reading

From observation and from talking to children about books and reading, it did seem that their interest and enthusiasm had grown. More children were visiting the library regularly. Children were more able to express their preferences for, and choice of, books and authors.

During the quiet reading sessions, children were quicker to organise themselves and become absorbed in their reading.

Failing readers

The attitude of this group of failing readers was certainly changing. On coming to the school they were very much concerned with progressing 'up the ladder' of particular reading schemes. Due to their poor self-image they would often choose 'hard' and, for them, unreadable books to be seen with at reading times. They placed no value at all on story or meaning, just on reaching the end of a book and moving to another one.

These children would often scour the bookshelves immediately prior to reading times and take a pile of books almost indiscriminately. These would be dispensed with in a few minutes of the reading time. It was obvious that they had little interest; stories had never been important to them.

A good variety of books, the use of listening/reading tapes and, overall, more experience of written texts did help them towards an attitude that was more conducive to success in reading. They were able to respond to story and meaning. They were pleased to dwell on a favourite book and to select books that they felt they could read.

Parental attitudes

Here there were definite indicators of change. There was better attendance at open evenings and on special occasions, such as the Diwali presentation and Christmas assembly. There was a very good response to a 'summer evening', which included a video showing aspects of school life. From home contacts, a small group of parents were helping on a regular basis in school.

As the year progressed, it was felt that the most valid kind of evaluation would include unbiased feedback from parents and children involved in the scheme. As a teacher would not be able to conduct a survey of this kind (parents are usually very anxious to respond positively to teachers' questions), the help of a primary advisory teacher, who was unknown at that time to parents and children, was enlisted. He conducted a series of semi-structured interviews centred on the scheme and the material used with a random sample of parents at home and with their child at school. The summarised results of this are shown in Figure 5.3 and Figure 5.4. The letters in the table refer to individual children. Child 'A' comes from family 'A', and so on.

Looking at these responses, it seems that in Question 4(b), reading silently was not seen as a useful activity for half of the parents in the sample, in fact it was the most 'unpopular' activity. This reaction may well be because parents cannot see their role very clearly here. There should probably have been discussions as to how parents might, themselves, read the same book as the child and talk about it with them.

Question 5, referring to home visits, drew an obviously favourable response. This, together with feedback from the actual visits, would seem to justify the time spent.

Question 7 elicited a very definite response and would seem to indicate that the scheme was viewed favourably overall by parents.

The children's responses were also generally favourable, with perhaps a little more 'caution'.

The reservations about the food pack were probably caused by the mapping activity. On reflection, this could well have been done collaboratively in the classroom. More interest in reading is often mentioned by the children. Perhaps child I's remark about 'getting more time with Mum' emphasises an important aspect of such a scheme.

SUMMARY AND CONCLUSIONS

It was felt at the end of the year that this was a worthwhile and valuable scheme. A good deal had been learnt and now there seemed as many

Figure 5.3   Results of interviews in the home-reading learning project

	(A)	(B)	(C)
1 Are parents in agreement with concept of working/ learning at home?	Yes	Yes	Yes
2 Do they help willingly?	Yes	Yes	Yes
3 Are they confident in role?	Yes	Yes – already helps in school	Yes – also learns from children
4 Kinds of work most useful: very useful/useful/not useful			
(a) Reading aloud	v.useful	v.useful	v.useful
(b) Reading silently	not useful	not useful	useful
(c) Try it again spelling list	v.useful	v.useful	v.useful
(d) Project sheets/packs	v.useful	v.useful	useful
(e) Listening/reading tapes	n/a (cass- ette broken)	useful – enjoyable	n/a
(f) Books with workcards/ worksheets	useful	useful but difficulty varied	v.useful
5 Is home visiting			
(a) appreciated	Yes		Yes
(b) useful	Yes, partic. appreciated instead of going to 'them' all the time – more formal when in sch.	Not really necessary as she helps frequently in school.	
6 Any suggested changes or other comments	None	More writing without copying.	None
7 Would parents like scheme extended into 2nd year?	Yes	V.positive yes. Does not feel as pressurised as in homework, that often has to be in next day.	Yes

(D)	(E)	(F)	(G)	(H)	(I)	(J)
Yes	Yes	Yes	Yes	Yes	Yes	Yes
Yes	Yes	Yes –. enjoyable	Yes – older sister helps as well	Yes	Yes	Yes
Yes	To a certain extent but sometimes wonders what to do.	Yes – helps teacher in sch. so can refer questions.	Yes	Yes – helps general conversation through topics introduced in project.	Yes	Yes
useful not useful useful	v.useful useful v.useful	useful useful not useful	v.useful not useful useful	v.useful useful useful	v.useful not useful useful	v.useful useful v.useful
useful n/a	useful v.useful	v.useful useful	useful not useful	v.useful not useful	useful useful: also involves yngr childn.	useful useful
useful	useful	v.useful: makes her think	useful	useful	v.useful	useful
v.import. as parents work long hours in business.	Yes Yes – would like more	Not necess. as she helps teacher in sch.	Yes Yes	No home visit	Yes Yes very	Yes v.much Yes
None	None	Spelling cld be harder – more comprehension wld be useful	None	Could inc. more local studies	More question sheets on reading	None
Def. yes	Yes	Yes: wld like extension into Maths	Yes	Def yes. It also helps other members of the family	Def Yes	Yes

Figure 5.4 Children's comments

(A) Sometimes likes it/sometimes not. Does not like drawing. Would like to carry on but not so often as Mum 'sometimes gets angry' because child 'muddles letters'.

(B) Really enjoys it. Spends about ½ to 1 hour. Has made him more interested in reading. Very enthusiastic to carry on next year.

(C) Mostly older sister helps but sometimes Dad. Spends about ½ hour. Is interested but sometimes bored. Did not seem wildly enthusiastic; would like to carry on next year but less frequently.

(D) Enjoys it but does not like too much as 'younger brother makes a fuss'. The work has helped but worksheet is sometimes too complicated (e.g. the one about food). It has encouraged interest in reading and 'would carry on if it is good.'

(E) Good. Really enjoyed it. Likes both Mum and Dad to help. Would like to carry on.

(F) Really liked it but not too much at a time. Sometimes a bit too easy but definitely would like to carry on.

(G) Both parents help and older sister. Too much time spent on it gets boring. Sometimes has to read hard books and too complicated worksheets (e.g. food project). Still wants to continue but not so much.

(H) Both Mum and Dad help. Likes it fairly well. Parents sometimes get angry. 'House' project was too difficult but it has encouraged reading and would like to continue.

(I) Both parents help. Likes it but sometimes too long. Mostly interesting. Dad thinks it good but Mum helps most and 'it's a good thing because I get more time with Mum'. Never used to read much but likes reading more now. Especially likes weekend work. Would like to continue.

(J) Mum helps. Sometimes good – sometimes not. Spends about the right amount of time – not sure if it helps him or not but thinks it may have made him more interested in reading. Not quite sure about carrying on but would do it 'if not too much work'.

---

questions as solutions. One could consider extending this kind of scheme into Maths work – for how long in children's schooling could one hope to keep parents involved, and what kind of involvement is appropriate at each stage and with different groups of parents and children? What happens if a whole school does not want to become involved? Is it valid for individual teachers to do this kind of work?

Parents need continuing support and encouragement – but so do teachers in this kind of extended role that carries more 'risks' than work within the classroom!

It is so difficult in an area like this to measure the return for time and effort expended. We are trying to initiate changes that have such long-term implications when we involve parents as partners. In the end it probably comes down to working on assumptions formed from successes in this area, and a conviction that this kind of work makes sense.

This chapter has been concerned with a case study of a home-reading/ learning scheme carried out for one year with first-year children and their parents in a middle school. In many home-reading schemes, younger children are involved and parents are usually asked to listen to children read at home and/or to share books with them. When children become fluent in their reading, this pattern of help is often not appropriate. Many teachers in junior and middle schools look then to ways in which parents can still collaborate with teachers. This scheme explored some of these ways, trying always to work on the principle of breaking down the boundaries of learning between home and school, so that the learning taking place in each situation can be related and reinforced.

6 Children with reading difficulties – how can parents help?

Up to this point we have been looking at the generality of readers and how parents can be invited to collaborate with teachers and share reading at home with their child on a regular and structured basis. This approach, as we have seen, takes an important step further than the widespread but unstructured practice of children taking books home from school. When teachers plan and implement schemes in a thoughtful way, regarding parents as partners in the reading venture, they can be instituting quite profound changes in the relationship between home and school.

This chapter aims to do two things. The main aim is to describe and discuss some published projects based on paired reading, where children with a reading difficulty have been helped at home. The secondary aim is to present two different models of reading. The way in which teachers perceive reading will influence and inform not only their work with children in school, but also the role they ask parents to play. Some mention is made in this context of the kind of help children experiencing difficulty may receive in school. Here again we go back to our perceptions of reading.

Although the chapter looks specifically at children with reading difficulties, it is not concerned with the aetiology of such difficulties. Many books have been written on this theme, but the medical 'deficiency' model does not seem appropriate or helpful here. Many teachers have doubts about using the term 'dyslexia', which indicates that there is a fixed group of symptoms which, when most or all are present, may be classified as a syndrome and named as a condition from which some children suffer. Use of this term may be comforting in the sense that parents and children who have been bewildered and confused over the child's lack of progress in reading and writing are reassured that the child is neither lazy nor unintelligent. Conversely, labelling children can categorise them as being outside the provision of help available in mainstream school. Where outside assistance *is* available, the responsibility for these children may be transferred, and the children themselves may then receive fragmented guidance and help with their considerable and distressing difficulties.

WHICH MODEL OF READING?

Before proceeding any further, we will now look at the two models of reading. It is worth spending some time as teachers trying to decide how we perceive reading. Do we view reading as a part of the whole language development in a child – as an holistic process where the whole cannot be explained by analysing its component parts – or do we see reading as being made up of a series of separate, hierarchical skills which can be built up to make a whole? K. Goodman (1982) writes that 'Reading is less a series of hierarchical skills than a psycholinguistic guessing game.'

The concept we have of reading will not only influence the way in which we teach or enable children to learn, it will also inform the way in which we ask parents to collaborate with us. This is important both for children whose early experiences of reading follow a smooth pattern and for children who find reading difficult.

It would seem useful here to look at each model in more detail in order to tease out its implications for working with children and with parents. Models are hypothetical mental constructs and it is improbable that anyone would follow a model exclusively and dogmatically in real life. Models are useful, however, for showing us what we feel to be nearest our own way of thinking.

1 Skills model

This is a 'bottom up' approach to reading. Reading is broken down into its smallest component parts, which are then studied and synthesised into larger components and gradually, like building up a wall, the final product is realised. There are two main routes within the skills model of reading: (a) the phonic approach and (b) the look and say approach.

(a) *The phonic approach*
In this approach, letter to sound correspondence is taught; the teacher presenting groups of letters with their associated sounds in progressing levels of difficulty. There are several considerable disadvantages with this approach, as Frank Smith points out in *Reading*. First, English is an alphabetic and *not* a phonetic language. We have 44 sounds for our twenty-six letters. According to Frank Smith, in order for children to be able to make a phonic approach work for them, they would have to master 166 rules and many exceptions. Added to this, most of the more common words are exceptions. This expectation is obviously unrealistic, especially on the part of young inexperienced readers. The actual concept of letter to sound correspondence is very difficult to grasp; it has no intrinsic meaning that children can bring their considerable experience in language to bear upon. Separate components are always more difficult to comprehend than whole entities. Imagine learning to ride a bicycle or to swim by studying each movement required separately and perfectly before being allowed to sit on the bicycle or enter the water!
Many parents and teachers say that they remember being taught like this. They can now read effectively, so, therefore, it must have been a good enough way to learn. It is likely, though, that at the same

time as they were being presented with phonics, they were also learning about reading in other ways. They were looking at books, hearing stories read and told, being read with, and all the time trying to extract sense from the world of print that daily surrounds us. The reason that some people recollect their phonics teaching may be because of the difficulty they experienced with it.

(b) *Look and say approach*

In this method, reading is approached by teaching children to recognise and pronounce individual words. Words are memorised from their visual configuration. In this approach, the first words taught are 'key' words which will form the vocabulary of the first reader. Most of the child's reading at the early stages will come from a reading scheme with a strictly controlled vocabulary, repeating words and using short, simple sentences.

In both the phonic and the look and say approaches (adherents to the skills-based model of reading often use a mixture of both), meaning is attended to after sufficient numbers of words and sounds have been learnt. Although breaking down a complex process into its smallest components in order to learn about the process seems logical, this is not the way in which language works. Children learn to read in much the same way as they learn to talk, and if we consider that idea then we will look for ways to give children plenty of experience of reading and books, put them in close contact with fluent readers and reading matter which is interesting and important.

2   The process model of reading

If we approach reading using this model, we will look at and try to understand the whole picture of reading and the various cognitive processes that take place in the brain in order that we can read. It is from this understanding that we would help children to *learn* to read – rather than *teach* them through rather difficult and abstract processes.

If we subscribe to the process model, we will think of children learning to read much as they learned to talk – by being read to and by joining in the reading, by trying to make sense out of the written language that surrounds them and always endeavouring to make meaning.

From studying fluent readers, it seems that the most powerful strategy a reader can use is prediction in the context of meaning and knowledge of language. Kenneth Goodman (1982) refers to reading as 'the psycholinguistic guessing game'. In the search for meaning, we will not insist that young readers achieve word for word accuracy. The reader – the 'apprentice' reader – will also bring meaning *to* the text as well as extracting meaning *from* the text. By bringing meaning to the text, as Frank Smith explains in *Reading*, the reader can load the 'trade off' between visual information (the text) and non-visual information (the theory of the world inside the mind of the reader). When a good balance is achieved, the reader can cope with the load of information from reading coming into short-term memory, and not be overwhelmed by it.

Bringing meaning to the text is achieved by the child having some considerable previous knowledge about what they are about to read. This knowledge can come immediately from having talked about a story or by having had the book read to them. Less immediately, young children have a considerable implicit knowledge of language, how books and stories work, and that the language of books is different from the spoken word. All this experience can be gained at home with parents as well as more formally at school.

Whichever model of reading the teacher or school chooses, it will affect the way in which they ask parents to co-operate. For example, if teachers subscribe to a skills model, they will advise parents to encourage children to 'sound out' unknown words. If a process model, parents will be asked to encourage children to look at the context of the meaning of the word first, or to go on and then come back, or for the parent to supply the word so that the fluency and, therefore, the meaning can be maintained.

If teachers follow a skills model, they may emphasise parents' accuracy rather than fluency. If such children are building up a 'memory bank' of individual words or sounds, then parents may be asked to go through these with the child to increase the number of times the child is exposed to each word or sound. In such a skills model of reading, parents might be asked to hear a child read a certain number of pages rather than share together a complete story or episode in a story. The books that a child takes home in a skills-based context will probably be of structured reading material, usually from a reading scheme. In a process-based context, the child might well be selecting books from a collection of individual titles. It might also be that parents are encouraged more to listen to the child read in a skills-based context than to share reading with the child.

Real difficulties might arise if the teachers' and parents' model of reading were different. The child might then become confused.

THE RELATIONSHIP BETWEEN PARENT, CHILD, TEACHER AND SCHOOL

Before going on to describe and discuss the technique of paired reading, let us look at the picture of the parent, child and teacher against the background of the school. One thing of which we can be certain is that there will be a high degree of anxiety in all three parties because of past feelings of frustration and failure, and present fears of future failure and the long-term consequences.

Parents and teachers will talk about children falling behind as they go through the junior school because so much of their learning is based on the written word. This is increasingly the case in secondary school, not only because of the importance of the written word, but also because, looking at the size of the school and the number of teachers, parents feel that their child's needs cannot possibly be met adequately or sympathetically.

The organisation and timetabling of most secondary schools also makes learning especially difficult for these children, as the learning activities are subject-based with abrupt changes to different subjects perhaps six or seven times a day. The different subject teachers may not always be prepared or able to give extra help and support.

As a solution, such children may find themselves in a smaller class of children who all have learning difficulties and who will follow a modified curriculum at a slower pace than their peers. This is certainly a solution, but has the important disadvantage of giving limited expectations on the part of the school and consequently limited performance and achievement from the child. So the downward spiral proceeds.

Of course, young children themselves do not hold this long-term and gloomy prospect in their minds; they are concerned with immediate events. What they *can* see, however, is that their classmates are able to read and enjoy books and material that they cannot and that their parents are anxious and perhaps impatient over their reading difficulty.

When teachers have considered the parents of these children, they have seen obstacles in the way of inviting them to collaborate in a programme of help. Teachers are aware of the anxiety of parents and are concerned that such anxiety might make them impatient when working with their child. Teachers also might feel that the child would be distressed in such a situation, finding the pressure of a parent more difficult to bear than the more neutral attitude of the teacher. Looking at the other side of this argument, it could be said that anxiety feeds on inactivity, frustration and lack of understanding. If teachers can help parents to channel their anxiety and tension in constructive rather than destructive ways, then they not only enlist extra help for the child, but also succeed in removing some of the pressure from the situation.

Co-operation with such parents needs much care and sensitivity on the part of the teacher. Parents are often critical of the school, which they see to be responsible for their child's failure and it is difficult for teachers not to react defensively. On the contrary, parents of these children need extra encouragement, support and praise for their efforts because it is probable that they harbour deep feelings of guilt and failure in themselves.

REMEDIATION IN SCHOOL

It does sometimes happen in a school that children who are having difficulty with their reading spend less time with books, either real storybooks or books containing interesting information, than the vast majority of children who have become fluent and, consequently, experienced readers. Fluent readers can confidently choose their reading material and make it work for them. Faltering readers have neither independent access to such a wide range of reading, nor do they have confidence in themselves. Often they have never understood the reason for reading – never experienced satisfaction and pleasure in a text – and reading has never worked for them. Each fresh encounter with the reading task presents high risks of failure with no positive expectations to weigh against this risk.

It would seem that these children desperately need good experiences with books, which probably means that a good deal of their reading at this stage may need to be mediated by a more fluent and probably older, understanding reader.

What can happen, though, is that this group of children receive remedial help in the form of drills and exercises in what are seen to be the subskills of reading. These children may be withdrawn from the usual classroom activities, which may be justified when the situation is urgent. What happens once they are withdrawn is perhaps not so justifiable.

It seems that children who have not made a good start with reading, perhaps by trying to use a phonic or look and say approach, are presented with more of the same kind of teaching that they were not able to benefit from in the first place. Frank Smith argues that we often make learning to read difficult by trying to split up the whole into its component, separate but meaningless parts. Children who have made a poor start can spend valuable time and effort on activities which take them further and further away from contact with real books, the point and the end goal for their effort, but also the *means* by which they will gain more competence in reading.

It has been stated earlier that this chapter will not be looking at the aetiology of failure. It does seem that in much of the published literature about reading failure (which is greater in volume than that published about fluent readers) there is comparatively little consideration given to the effect of initial instruction in reading. Perhaps such a consideration would be more constructive than dwelling on the causes of failure, in that we might be more open to the idea that any fault or failing may not be with the reader but in the way in which we have approached reading. We might then look at our materials and method of instruction more closely.

PAIRED READING

This strategy for a reading dyad was first given prominence by Morgan and was based on principles of behavioural psychology. The behavioural aspect was built on the concept of participant modelling with reinforcement, but the benefits and gains from this method seem to be psycholinguistic rather than purely mechanical, because the model of reading underlying it is holistic rather than skills-based.

The procedure

1   The *child* chooses the reading material.
2   Child and adult (parent in this case) start reading aloud simultaneously. Accuracy is required. The parent has to find a suitable pace which enables the child to join in as much as possible, but still keeps the meaning of the text. It is here that the 'participant modelling' takes place as the child, while joining in the reading, can hear the parent providing a model for intonation and expression. The parent runs a finger under the line of text as the reading proceeds.
3   *Independent reading by child*   The child makes a pre-arranged signal to indicate that he/she is going to read independently. The parent gives very frequent praise as reward for attempting to read independently.
4   *Error made by child*   The parent corrects the error without comment and now parent and child resume simultaneous reading.

The cycle starts again. The aim is to encourage the child into more sustained periods of independent reading. This is done by the lack of adverse comment and the frequent praise for any independent reading.

In their article in the *Association of Educational Psychologists' Journal* and in *Parental Involvement in Children's Reading*, describing research carried out in Derbyshire, Bushell *et al.* (1982, 1985) see forces other than behavioural ones at work in paired reading. They see the enhancement of the child's self-esteem, together with the practice of the child choosing the reading material, as being the trigger to the psycholinguistic processes.

Failure, which has been the child's shadow up to now, is eliminated in this practice. Added to this, the pupil (child) and tutor (parent) start this new way of reading together at the same time. They receive instruction together and both have an equal part to play. The situation is novel for both of them, which helps give the practice a positive start. The flow of meaning from the text is maintained as the child does not have to pause and find new words.

The flow and fluency of reading is important to children experiencing difficulty; they can thereby make use of contextual cues rather than just graphic-phonic ones.

WHY ARE PARENTS THE BEST PARTNERS IN THE PRACTICE OF PAIRED READING?

Most of the projects written up about paired reading have been based on the dyad of parent and child. In some projects teachers have partnered children as a comparison or as an alternative, but usually the results of these pairings are not so good. This is probably because of the different relationship between the partners and the fact that school is not as conducive as home to relaxed reading.

Parents make better partners in this kind of project because:

1 they have a unique concern for their own child;
2 the context of the reading takes place in the relatively unhurried atmosphere of home;
3 the 'package' as presented to parents and children has definite, simple steps to follow;
4 the practice is very 'labour intensive' (in most projects the reading takes place every evening) and therefore is difficult to implement in school;
5 the practice presents a positive way of diverting parents' underlying anxiety into constructive effort.

A DESCRIPTION OF A PROJECT USING PAIRED READING

One of the earliest projects in paired reading was that carried out in Derbyshire by Bushell *et al.* (1982, 1985). The researchers, A. Miller, R. Bushell and D. Robson, were at that time educational psychologists in that county and worked in collaboration with teachers and schools in the area.

Their research was carried out in three main stages: a pilot study, a main study and a third phase where schools were encouraged to take over the initiative. Up to this point the researchers had instructed parents and visited and advised them at home. In the main study there were two groups of children, a group who took part in paired reading and a control group. After the experiment had run for six weeks, the control group themselves took part in paired reading so that three sets of results were obtained. Neale's *Analysis of Reading Ability* was used before and after the intervention as a measure of reading gains.

The steps followed in the paired reading were those identified earlier in the chapter, and the total average reading time over the six weeks was 7.6 hours. The results of Neale's *Analysis of Reading Ability* showed significant and sometimes dramatic gains, mainly in accuracy rather than in comprehension. The results of a standardised test carried out before and after such a short period of intervention must be open to question, as the researchers themselves suggest, but this and other projects have included supporting qualitative data.

The researchers were able to conclude that the following three elements of paired reading necessary for its success:

1 Simultaneous reading where both parent and child feel comfortable needs to be established.
2 Increasingly long periods of independent reading have to be aimed for.
3 The transition from the child reading independently back to simultaneous reading should be smooth.

From the project it was found that when children had a free choice of material, they quite quickly adjusted to selecting 'reasonable' books. This seems to imply that children tended to choose books at their 'instructional' level, which of course would mean more chance of independent reading.

The role of the teacher was seen to be crucial, whether the school initiated a scheme or collaborated with another agency. Findings from similar projects have stressed this; terms such as warm, welcoming, valuing, sensitive and supporting are used. The researchers also felt that teachers should be willing to go and see parents at home.

Support from the LEA is again seen as useful and important. Working with parents and children in paired reading is much more time-consuming than a more generalised home-reading scheme. Time can be saved by drawing together groups of parents for instruction, but if, for instance, schools can be allowed time for home visits, schemes are likely to be more effective.

Other projects, some of which are described in *Parental Involvement in Children's Reading* (Topping and Wolfendale, 1985), have similar ingredients and have shown positive and hopeful indicators in their results.

SUMMARY AND CONCLUSIONS

It seems that many paired reading projects have been initiated by educational psychologists, either within an LEA or in a university. In the longer term the main responsibility for this kind of activity probably needs to be based in schools with teachers. This is becoming more and more the case, with other agencies offering external support and consultancy.

As with all schemes where teachers and parents collaborate, the effects are likely to be wider than just an improvement in reading. Parents are anxious about their child's lack of progress and perhaps critical of what they see to be the school's failure. Children are handicapped in most areas of their learning and excluded from the 'reading community'. To be able to turn this situation around is very satisfying and must change the feelings of child and parent about schooling.

Teachers who organise a paired reading project have a much more concentrated part to play than in the more generalised home-reading scheme. At the very least they need to be accessible and, ideally, ready to go and talk to parents at home. Great sensitivity is needed by teachers working in this way.

Most projects in paired reading tend to be fairly short and intensive. The technique would seem to produce an initial reversal of previous patterns of failure and frustration. A period of paired reading can serve as a boost to the child's interest and enjoyment in reading. Subsequently, a 'softer', more gradual approach, as in the shared reading of a home-reading scheme, could be used to sustain the interest and improvement in reading and to keep parents and teachers in touch. It may be that a school which is starting or developing a home-reading scheme might try paired reading with a few of its children who are having difficulty with reading, alongside its more general approach with the majority of the children.

One note of warning must be sounded. From the various projects which have been carried out, it seems that almost all parents can be involved in a partnership scheme and work in this close and concentrated way with their child. There must be some exceptions to this situation and these would occur when there are real difficulties at home based on a temporary crisis or more prolonged emotional disturbance. In this situation, it would be unwise to attempt this kind of work as it would be putting added stress into an already fragile situation. In extreme situations, school is a refuge and bringing the two worlds together is not in the best interests of the child. This is where outside agencies could be consulted and perhaps alternative plans put into operation. The work of voluntary reading helpers in school, which might provide a viable alternative, is discussed in the next chapter.

The actual practice of paired reading, although based on behavioural principles, follows an holistic model of reading. Concentration is not placed on isolated subskills, but on meaning and understanding.. Children who have difficulty with reading build up a set of enjoyable and satisfying experiences with texts and begin to see reading as readers do. They are starting to see the point of reading.

This chapter has been concerned with children who have reading difficulties and describes paired reading as a way in which their parents can help. It has also considered skills-based and process-based models of reading and the implications of each model as regards collaboration with parents. There has been a brief glance at how children who find reading difficult can be taken further away from books and reading while receiving remedial help in school.

SECTION III

This section of the book concentrates on the parent and child working together in the classroom.

7   Parents in school

In this chapter we move the focus from home to school and look at some research into the part that parents play within some schools, helping children with their reading. The chapter is based mainly on a research project carried out by Barry Stierer and recorded in his report to the Social Science Research Council, 'Parental Help with Reading in Schools Project'. There will be discussion and elaboration upon some of the findings from the writer's own experiences and contacts with teachers, parents and children.

Although the project was concerned with parents helping with reading in school, the basis of their work is very different from that in a home-reading situation with their own child.

'Clearly it is not the immediate parent-child "reading relationship" which determines the success of these schools' use of parent reading helpers' (Stierer, 1985). In many schools, as we shall see, parents were not acting in the role of parents but as adult voluntary reading helpers.

The practice of parents working in school raises more issues than that of reading with their child at home as part of a home-reading scheme. The dynamism is less simple and direct.

THE RESEARCH

The research referred to was carried out in three stages between 1983 and 1985. The design was as follows:

Stage 1:   Postal questionnaires (previously piloted) were sent out to a sample of five hundred primary schools in England.
Stage 2:   In-depth interviews were carried out with heads, teachers and parents in thirty selected schools.
Stage 3:   More prolonged visits were made to a few schools whose approach to working with parent-helpers was different from that of the majority of schools, which was based on reading aloud.

SOME FACTS AND FIGURES FROM THE POSTAL QUESTIONNAIRE

Out of the 500 schools which were sent questionnaires, 381 responded – a very high response rate of 76%. Out of those 381 schools, 202 (or 53%)

were asking volunteer helpers to help with reading in school on a regular basis. Within this number there were different categories of helpers: 39% of schools involved parents of children at the school only, 14% involved adults other than parents only, 47% involved a combination of parent and other helpers.

Surprisingly, it emerged that almost as many junior as infant schools were receiving outside help with reading.

The *number of parents* involved in each school varied tremendously. The average number of helpers per class was between two and three, with a few classes receiving help with reading regularly from as many as 20 parents.

In some schools not all the classes received help. There were more infant schools than junior schools where it was a whole-school policy to involve reading helpers (51% as compared with 35%).

The *length of time* worked by volunteer reading helpers varied considerably between and within schools. The average time given by individual helpers was around two hours per week, with some helpers giving four to five hours.

The *number of children* who read to the helper was usually five per hour, but in some cases helpers heard more than ten children in an hour.

Underneath these statistics there lies a fascinating variety of intention, thinking and practice.

What were the main aims of the schools who involved parent-helpers?

From the answers in the postal questionnaire and from subsequent discussions, two kinds of benefits were envisaged:

1 *Benefits that related directly to children's reading*
   These included improved reading performance; extra practice; being able to talk to an adult about reading; greater interest in reading.

2 *Benefits that were more indirect*
   These included the opportunity for children to have a one-to-one relationship with an adult other than the teacher in the classroom; parents gaining a better understanding of the reading process; parents knowing more about books; parents having a better appreciation of the aims of the school generally.

A factor that was often mentioned was that the 'open door' policy of a school could be put into practice by inviting parents to work with teachers.

WHAT DID PARENTS FEEL THEY GAINED FROM HELPING WITH READING IN THE CLASSROOM?

This question was not asked in the postal questionnaire, but it was interesting when talking to parents regularly involved in reading to try to find out why they agreed to help and what benefits they felt *they* had gained from being involved.

First of all it seemed that some kind of consideration for their own child influenced their decision to offer their help. Parents felt that they could contribute in some way to their child's education, though not as directly as through reading with their child at home. They felt they could help their child if they gained a better understanding of the reading process by joining in what was going on in school. They hoped to use this understanding when reading with the child at home and also when they tried to help any older or younger children. A few parents stated that an older child had experienced difficulty with reading so they offered to help in school in order to be able to help the younger child and guarantee that this child would not suffer in the same way.

A simpler and more direct motivation for offering help was that parents were pressurised into it by the child who wanted them to come into school.

Some parents of young children said that they wanted to come into school so that they could join in, to a certain extent, with their child's new experience of school. They did not want to 'hand their child over' to the teacher.

Having once established themselves and gained some confidence in the classroom, parents would then start to take a real interest in the group of children with whom they regularly worked. Most parents committed themselves to help for a year so they were able to see the children develop as readers. They would comment with satisfaction not only on the children's progress, as they saw it, but also on their increasing confidence, interest and real enjoyment of reading.

Parents who had been working with children experiencing difficulty showed particular interest and satisfaction. They talked about their sense of achievement when a child started to 'take off' with their reading. These remarks were surprising as some of these parents did not work at all with their own child in school.

Parents often expressed spontaneously their own enjoyment of many of the books they shared with children, commenting, 'I don't remember books being like that when I was at school.'

Reflecting on what they thought they had gained from being a reading helper, some parents stated that they had become aware of their own child's capability in relation to the other children in the class and had realised that their child behaved in a much more independent and responsible way than they did at home!

If the school included in its aims that of gaining the appreciation and understanding of its parents, then that aim was certainly realised. Parents volunteered their admiration for the class teacher, mainly for her patience, resourcefulness, organisation and general good humour.

WERE PARENT-HELPERS SELECTED IN ANY WAY?

The question of whether a school accepted all offers of help with reading or whether they 'chose' parents was discussed. When a school decided to involve parent-helpers with reading many different arrangements were used.

In some schools there was no open and general invitation, but rather individual requests to parents whom the teachers or head already knew. Sometimes heads contacted parents directly or passed on names of 'approved' parents to teachers.

Schools sometimes found themselves in a dilemma because on the one hand they wanted to promote the 'openness' of the school and on the other hand they were apprehensive of finding themselves with 'unsuitable' help in the sensitive area of reading. One solution was for the school, or the individual class teacher, to offer a variety of tasks needing help – swimming, cooking, library, craft activities – as well as reading. Parents would then self-select for the different tasks depending upon their own strengths and the times when they were available. If a teacher and a parent could not work together well, as did happen occasionally, then the parent was tactfully redirected to another task such as helping in the library.

Another form of selection occurs when a school decides not to invite any parents to help with reading on the grounds of what the school perceives as their general unsuitability. A discussion of some of the reasons why schools did not invite parental help will be found later in this chapter.

DID PARENTS WORK WITH THEIR OWN CHILDREN?

This was one of the questions included in the postal survey. The underlying reasons for the answers given were followed up in subsequent interviews. In a large number of the schools which responded to the survey, parents did not work with their own child. This raises again the question of parents not carrying through any parental role, but rather being seen as keen, but disinterested, adult helpers.

There were two main reasons given for not arranging for parents to work with their own child:

1 Parents were specifically assigned to work with a certain category of reader to which their own child did not belong, for example fluent readers, or readers who were experiencing considerable difficulty.

2 It was feared that the child would feel embarrassed or 'act up' so the contact was deliberately avoided.

In some instances the result of this arrangement was that parents did not work within their child's class, but in the school as a whole. The strongest forms of collaboration, though, seem to be based around the class teacher working with a group of parents. This gives parents a sense of identity and purpose.

Young children and their parents on various occasions expressed surprise that mother and child did not work together in school. As one mother said, 'He would be very put out if I didn't read with him!' It might be that older, junior age children would feel rather self-conscious initially, but this feeling rarely persists.

WHICH CATEGORY OF READERS DID PARENTS WORK WITH?

The most usual category of reader was the group of children who had become quite fluent in their reading. Here teachers placed emphasis on extra practice and the opportunity to share books with an interested adult for a sustained and uninterrupted period. In such situations it was stressed by heads and teachers that parents were in no way acting as teachers as there was no teaching involved in this activity.

There was, however, a minority category including beginning readers and, perhaps more controversially, older children who were having difficulty with reading. It was very interesting to realise that schools were using opposite sides of the same argument to reflect their concern for their children who were struggling with reading. Some schools argued that these children needed the specialist help of a qualified teacher and would not involve parents. Other schools argued that these children needed so much help, attention and opportunity to read that they had priority when extra help was available. A third group of schools, which involved qualified teachers as voluntary helpers, directed them to this category of reader, while asking non-teaching parents to listen to their more fluent readers.

WHAT DID PARENTS ACTUALLY DO?

Barry Stierer, in his report to the Education and Human Development Committee of the Social Science Research Council, divides up the kind of help that parents gave into two categories – a 'majority' practice which was based on listening to children read and a 'minority' practice based on other kinds of help.

The 'majority' practice – listening to children read

There were variations within this activity, but it proceeded mainly as follows:

Parent-helpers listened to children read on a one-to-one basis under the supervision of the class teacher. They would read with the same children each time they came into school. They tended to work with the more fluent readers. Teachers saw this kind of reading as practice and were willing to devolve what they saw as an onerous but necessary task to helpers.

It is interesting to consider this view in conjunction with some of the findings and recommendations emerging from *Extending Beginning Reading* (Southgate *et al.*, 1981) where the preoccupation and practice of teachers endeavouring to listen to children read aloud on a frequent and regular basis is looked at closely. It was found that the average 'effective' length of time in these circumstances was 30 seconds because of the constant interruptions from other children in the class. Added to this, the researchers commented on the diversionary activities taking place in the rest of the class at the times when individual oral reading was taking place.

Given the short bursts of time without interruption, the writers of that book concluded that it was impossible to attend to the main concerns in working with individual readers, which are: diagnosis, assessment, probing children's reading strategies, and discussion of the book and of the process of reading.

It is also interesting to note that one of the conclusions arrived at from the classes surveyed was that the children who made the most progress in reading over the year of the research were in classes where the teacher placed the least emphasis on children's oral reading.

It appeared from Barry Stierer's research that often helpers were spending more time with individual children on reading than was their teacher. This could have had far-reaching implications as it might have been that the parents' model of reading was having a greater influence on the child than that of the teacher. Where the teacher and parent helper are collaborating closely with good feedback, consultation and understanding, they will have the same perspective on reading and will be reinforcing the same model. However, in a few schools parents do not work in the classroom, but in a corridor or spare room, and there is little consultation and feedback. In these situations children may be receiving confusing messages, for instance on the question as to whether accuracy or meaning is more important.

Occasionally, in some schools parents are expected, or feel they are expected, to 'get through' a considerable number of children reading to them. A production line technique operates with the child being briskly withdrawn from an interesting activity in the classroom, locating the parent-helper in the corridor, waiting for their turn to read, opening the book and reading without any discussion, reading the statutory two pages and then being signed off and deputed to go and fetch the next child on the list.

Another issue relating to the practice of reading aloud to parent-helpers is this: Should all instances of reading aloud be for diagnostic purposes? If this is so, where does this place the parent? Teachers and heads emphasised the role of the parent as being that of providing mainly a 'listening ear'. If this is so, the material being read must be seen as self-teaching, i.e. a structured and controlled reading scheme. Frequent reading from this kind of material can enhance mechanical decoding skills at the expense of reading for meaning. If reading aloud is regarded as being a valuable way of gaining insight into what children are making of the reading process, how can we give this task to untrained helpers rather than to professional teachers?

It might be that when more fluent readers are frequently asked to read aloud, their development as readers could be held back rather than advanced. Schools who can appreciate the wider benefits of opening up classrooms to parents may view this practice as simple and straightforward. If schools could give some time and thought to how parent-helpers might be most effective, they might help parents to operate in small discussion groups about books, share books with individual children, help and talk about choosing books, and keep the reading aloud, perhaps, for selected extracts. Reading aloud is more difficult than reading silently when it comes to working with the meaning of the text.

The 'minority' practices

We turn now from the widely accepted but by no means straightforward model of reading aloud, to look at some more unusual models which were followed up in the last stage of the research.

1   A workshop approach
This model is based on parents working in the classroom with their own child. One of its benefits is that it resolves the paradox of parents not acting as parents when they come into school. Briefly, the teacher prepares and organises reading and language related activities for parent and child to work on together, trying to involve all parents on a regular basis. The organisational and time factors here are considerable and because of this it might happen that the activities are at a rather low level of usefulness. A fuller description of this way of working is given in the next chapter, when the Foxhill Reading Project is described.

2   Supplementing a home-reading scheme
There are some schools which run a home-reading scheme but do not generally involve parents in school. In a few of these schools parents are specifically involved in reading with children whose own parents have not joined in the scheme. These schools do not imagine that they can reproduce the dynamic processes at work in the close bonding of parent and child at home, but rather seek to compensate for the child's feeling of isolation. Parent-helpers in these circumstances work exclusively with these children on a regular basis.

3   Running induction courses
A few schools had managed to make time for and given considerable effort to, running extended courses for parents on many aspects of the curriculum. Subsequently, parents were invited to help in various activities in the school, including reading. It was found that the help that these parents were able to give was of a high quality and the participants felt that the time given to the courses was well spent. The benefits were seen to operate both in school and at home as well, as parents became more confident in their role as educators.

SCHOOLS WHICH DID NOT INVOLVE PARENT-HELPERS

The postal survey and subsequent discussions tried to establish why some schools (47%) of the sample) did not invite parent-helpers into school to assist with children's reading. In one-third of these schools the question of whether to involve adult helpers had not been raised. This did not necessarily mean that the schools disapproved of involving parents with reading, as some of them did in fact encourage parents to read with children at home.

The schools who had decided not to invite adult helpers to assist with reading were subdivided into two groups – one group which had never involved helpers in this way and the other group which had used reading helpers but had discontinued the practice.

WHY SOME SCHOOLS NEVER INVOLVED PARENT-HELPERS

There were three main reasons that were cited:

1 'Drawing the line at reading'

These schools regarded every aspect of learning to read as needing the skill of a professionally trained teacher. While these schools often stated that they involved parents in other areas of the curriculum, such as cooking and craftwork, they drew the line at reading:

> 'It is the feeling of the staff that hearing children read should always be diagnostic and that untrained helpers do not have the expertise to apply diagnostic methods and follow them up.'

> 'Every aspect of reading development requires specialist application. Satisfactory progress can only be achieved by using excellent teachers. I should also refuse major surgery from a hospital porter.'

Conversely, though, schools who did involve adult reading helpers saw reading as being too vital to be left solely to the hard-pressed class teacher.

2 The parents

Many schools stated that they did not feel that the parents in their catchment area would be able to make a viable contribution to children's reading. Factors such as having little English, having a low level of literacy and having difficult domestic circumstances were cited.

Conversely, again, schools who did involve parent-helpers in similar areas emphasised that one of the main reasons for doing so was to try to bring such parents into the school community and to encourage their participation in their children's learning.

3 Lack of reading problems/many reading problems

Both these reasons were given for not asking parents to help. Some schools stated that they were so satisfied with the children's level of reading attainment that they did not feel they needed any outside assistance. On the other hand, schools who stated that they had a large number of children experiencing reading difficulties gave this as the reason for not inviting outside help as they felt that this would do more harm than good.

Conversely, some schools who did use outside help did so precisely on account of their children having reading difficulties.

Other much less common reasons for not involving parent-helpers included: a lack of whole-school consensus, a fear of lack of confidentiality, and parental opposition.

WHY SOME SCHOOLS DISCONTINUED THE PRACTICE OF INVOLVING PARENT-HELPERS

By far the most common reason given for discontinuing the practice was that the helpers' children had left the school or that helpers had taken up paid employment and were no longer available. The fact that these schools had not tried to replace their volunteer helpers indicates that they were probably not strongly committed to the idea.

Much less commonly cited reasons for discontinuing a scheme were: misgivings about the ways in which parents were working, a very few instances of a break in confidentiality and the need for outside help becoming alleviated by a reduction in class sizes.

The National Union of Teachers, in its booklet *Home/School Relations and Adults in Schools* (1983) raises some questions about adult helpers and refers specifically to help with children's reading. The union sees the practice of oral reading to have important diagnostic purposes, and comments on parents' lack of expertise in this area. It is particularly concerned with the involvement of parent-helpers with children who are experiencing reading difficulties.

The union is particularly concerned, also, with the inexperienced teacher, who it contends 'needs professional support, not a band of well-meaning volunteers'. It fears that such teachers may feel pressurised into accepting parental help when they would rather decline. This point is returned to in Chapter 9.

As has been discussed, all of the reasons for not involving parents in assisting children's reading in school have their counter arguments. A very strong feature of the research was the pronounced differences in thinking and the strength of feeling with which teachers held their convictions. One argument, though, is difficult to answer, and this was mentioned many times in the survey, in subsequent interviews and in other contacts with heads and teachers. This was: should schools involve outside helpers to compensate for any kind of shortfall of staff which might have arisen through cut-backs in finance?

SUMMARISING THE FINDINGS AND RAISING SOME ISSUES

The importance of reading in the curriculum

From Stierer's initial survey, from interviews and from discussions with heads and teachers, parents and children, there comes a picture in which there is no doubt about the primacy given to reading in the curriculum. It is because reading is seen to be of paramount importance that some schools are anxious to enlist the help of volunteers and other schools are anxious to make reading the sole preserve of qualified and experienced teachers. Yet other schools see reading as not only vitally important in its own right, but also as a focus for collaboration between parents and teachers to bring about a more open school.

Reasons for introducing voluntary help schemes

Some schools have introduced voluntary help schemes with reading as a direct or indirect response to a withdrawal of remedial help in the school. Although voluntary helpers may not work alongside children experiencing reading difficulty, they may relieve the teacher of the task of listening to children read and free her to devote more time to these children.

A feeling of compromise

Many heads feel compromised by having to involve voluntary helpers in situations where they may be compensating for the lack of paid teaching staff. This is an especially sensitive point when schools involve qualified unemployed teachers as volunteers. This dilemma is intractable; as one head teacher argued, 'I know that I am replacing missing staff with volunteer help and papering over the cracks, but I can't stand by and see children lose out while we wait for things to improve.'

An enrichment, not a compensation

Many schools have had voluntary reading help schemes in operation for some years and many more schools set up such schemes in the conviction that they will bring added benefits, and not as a compensatory device. Teachers see the gains in children's reading and the positive attitudes brought about by collaboration as a new and significant dimension in their teaching.

A widening gap between schools?

If schools in predominantly middle-class areas are involving more parent-helpers than in working-class areas, then the already considerable gap between some schools may well be widened. This can be seen in some instances where PTAs in relatively affluent areas are supplying equipment and facilities to enhance the education of their children.

An erosion or extension of teachers' professionalism?

A few schools saw the presence of voluntary reading helpers in their classrooms as an erosion of their professionalism. They felt that parents might be taking over their role as teachers of reading. A growing number of teachers, however, see this kind of collaboration as a new direction for and an extension of their professional role. Working with other adults certainly requires additional organisation. Communicating with helpers requires a different kind of perspective and well-developed interpersonal skills.

Ingredients for success

It is not surprising to find that where there is a good deal of consultation, guidance and explanation there seems to be the most benefit to children's reading and the most satisfaction for the parents, children and teachers concerned. Time, patience and commitment are needed and where teachers are able to give these there will be a successful partnership between parents and teachers in school.

Reading aloud

The practice of oral reading by children to parent-helpers may need to be examined critically to see if it is the most effective way of using the time and expertise of the helpers.

SUMMARY

This chapter has been based on recent research about voluntary help with reading in school. The practice raises a number of complex issues and is not as straightforward as one in which parents collaborate with teachers in a home-reading scheme. There are many differences of opinion in this area, but where parent-helpers are not being used in the place of teachers, there seems little doubt that there is much benefit to be gained by all involved.

8 Three different ways of involving parents in the classroom

The previous chapter discussed recent research concerned with parent reading helpers in the classroom. This chapter begins by presenting briefly a case study of a typical collaboration between a teacher and a group of mothers in an Outer London school. It goes on to describe a well-known project involving parents in a classroom workshop and concludes with a discussion of some contemporary work in Inner London, based on the idea of parents as authors.

A TYPICAL PICTURE OF COLLABORATION IN THE CLASSROOM

It is nine o'clock in an infant classroom in a school in Outer London. Twenty-eight five, six and seven year-olds – mixed middle and top infants – and three or four mothers are waiting for the teacher to finish the 'business' of the morning. When this is finished, the children settle themselves down for their daily time with books and reading.

Many of the mothers of children in this class come into school regularly. The teacher is very committed to collaborating with parents in children's learning and has been opening her classroom to parents for some years.

At the beginning of the year all the parents were invited by the teacher to come and help with some of the classroom activities. These included reading, craftwork, projects, computer work and games. Parents were notified of the times of all these activities and those who wanted to help volunteered for an activity and a time which suited them. The mothers in the classroom on this particular morning chose reading.

All the children in the class spend the first half an hour of each day with books – reading to themselves, looking through picture books, reading in small groups with the teacher or with a mother, writing about or drawing what they have read, choosing and talking about books, or listening to a story on tape while reading the book.

The children are scattered round and beyond the room. Some are on the big floor cushions in the book corner, some are at their tables, some around the teacher. One or two might be in the adjoining hallway constructing a big pucture showing an arresting scene from a book they have just read. Another small group might be in the hall sharing a story (each of them having individual copies) with a mother.

The children are almost all committed readers with decided preferences

The children are scattered round the room.

in their reading and able to talk about what they appreciate or dislike in a book. The mothers read with the same children each time, mostly once a week, though a few mothers come in twice a week.

Mostly the helpers read and talk with individual children while the teacher works with a small group, sharing and discussing their reading. This arrangement is flexible, though, and changes from time to time. One mother, for instance, may work with just two children over the space of half an hour. She will read and talk about a picture-story book to each child individually. The mother and child will then share the reading and conclude with more talk, the mother offering much praise and mother will make brief comments in her record book, which the teacher keeps alongside her own.

The teacher regularly makes some time available for feedback, apart from the very brief exchanges with each parent after the session. Sometimes some parents stay on in the classroom past the reading time to join in and help with writing, especially helping children who are still using the material in *Breakthrough to Literacy* (an initial approach to reading and writing, published by Longman). These helpers are now experienced in talking with children within the context of their reading and it is easy for them to use the same kind of approach to draw children out about their ideas for writing.

At morning break-time it is natural for the teacher and parents to have coffee in the staff room, where they can discuss the activities of the morning or talk more generally.

Some children are reading in small groups with the teacher or with a mother.

The children of these mothers are obviously pleased to see their mother working alongside the teacher. They refer to the children who read with her as 'my mum's group'. They know that their friends enjoy the time they spend with their mother and they themselves enjoy this contact in the classroom, which is very different from the reading they share at home. There is no embarrassment or 'playing up'; the situation is quite natural and taken for granted. Parents join in activities throughout the school and are valued for their unique contribution.

The mothers themselves express considerable satisfaction and enjoyment in what they are doing. They take a real interest in 'their group' of children and comment on the child's growing confidence and enjoyment of books. They themselves have come to appreciate many of the good children's books nowadays available and have their own favourites, like *The Very Hungry Caterpillar* and *Burglar Bill*.

Sometimes helpers and teachers stop to share a joke with each other, often with the children included. It is the relaxed, yet purposeful, atmosphere that is so striking. This comes from the helpers' confidence in themselves and in the teacher's appreciation of their contribution. The shared confidence comes partly from a good positive relationship, but it comes also from an accord in the way that parents and teacher perceive reading.

The teacher organises a strong and successful home-reading scheme. All the parents who join the scheme (which includes the helpers in the classroom) come to a meeting before the scheme starts. There are usually two meetings – one in an afternoon and one in an evening. While the afternoon meeting is going on the teacher's children join a colleagues's class. The meetings include tea and biscuits and opportunity for informal talk.

The main part of the meeting is taken up with an explanation of how the school perceives reading. The teacher starts with a 'put yourself in their place' approach, with the parents joining in, all trying to read a short passage which has various parts missing to see what clues and what strategies they use. The points that the teacher makes are:

1 that prediction is a strong strategy and guessing within the context of meaning should be positively encouraged;

2 that a phonic approach is difficult and confusing and is only useful after the alternatives have been narrowed down;

3 that the enjoyment and pleasure in reading a variety of books and other material is vital. Without this children will not become committed or effective readers;

4 that real books with real stories are preferable to controlled reading scheme material;

5 that talking about the book and perhaps reading it to the child first is a good thing before the child reads aloud. When the child is reading aloud it is often good to share the reading;

6 that fluent readers do not need to read aloud very often and parents could share reading in a different way with them. This will be discussed at a later meeting;

7 that they as parents have a unique contribution to make to children's reading – not as a teacher but as a concerned adult who knows the importance of reading.

The teacher's approach is fairly forthright for she is convinced of her stance on reading. She does discuss various aspects with parents individually throughout the year, but at this first meeting the message is clear. She does not want parents to approach reading with their child from a skills base, but more from an 'apprenticeship' approach.

Some time after the introductory meeting, parents expressed their surprise and interest in how reading was being approached now. 'When we were at school it was all phonics and sounding it out.' Few parents had pleasant recollections of their earliest reading experiences. What the teacher had been explaining and demonstrating had been a revelation to them.

So parents and teacher are working together with mutual regard. Children benefit considerably from having other adults with whom they can read and talk.

Not all teachers welcome parents into the classroom, though. There are reasons for this:

Firstly – There are time and organisational factors which have to be considered. In the brief case study just considered, the arrangements were fairly straightforward and, as the collaboration proceeds, parents become more confident and need less guidance. Time and thought always need to be given for good consultation and feedback if a scheme is to be successful. In the kind of classroom workshop described below (at Foxhill) there is even more time and effort needed for preparation and follow up.

Secondly – There is a feeling that teachers' professionalism is being eroded and that parents might be making up for shortages in staffing provision. This has been discussed in the previous chapter. Where parents are an adjunct to, and not a necessary part of, the school's, resources then surely the practice can be seen as an enhancement of the role of the teacher – albeit in a different direction – rather than an erosion of it.

Thirdly – Some teachers feel that the most satisfactory learning group consists of a class of children and one teacher. They refer to the children as 'my children' and want to build up a close relationship with them as individuals and as a whole group. They feel that the presence of another adult dilutes and diverts the strong group feeling.

On the other hand, it has been shown, and common sense would suggest, that children benefit from talk and association with interested adults, both in and out of the classroom. Conventional classroom teaching can sometimes put pressure on a child who cannot respond wholeheartedly to the teacher's vision of group identity. Also, this kind of situation is not always a good basis for developing independence in learning.

FOXHILL READING WORKSHOP

A more unusual way of involving parents in school can be seen in the Foxhill project. This scheme, which is reported by Jo Weinberger in *Foxhill Reading Workshop*, was set up in 1981 with support from the Family Service Units organisation. Family Service Units is a national charity which seeks to improve the quality of life in run-down, inner city areas by building up community resources. The school, where the project ran initially for one year, is a nursery and infant school in Sheffield. The project aimed to involve parents with their own child in weekly workshops in the classroom. This collaboration acknowledged the dynamism of parent and child working together and answers some of the questions posed in cases where parents do not function within their parental role in school.

In the initial stage of the project, three groups of eight children aged five and six, from three different classes were brought together for an hour once a week under the supervision of the teacher/organiser to work with their own parent (in this case their mother). A crèche was available during this time.

The teacher prepared reading tasks, language games and worksheets beforehand. Parents looked over and discussed the plans over coffee as they arrived. While the workshop proceeded, the teacher encouraged and advised where needed. All the materials used in the workshop could be borrowed and used at home.

As the year went on, teachers visited parents at home to explain and advise, and to ascertain their feelings about the work. Irregular contributors to the workshop were encouraged to persevere. Parents who were unable to attend the workshop at school were visited once a fortnight and supplied with reading material and games to share with their child.

At the end of the first year, the participants were so pleased with the work that each class teacher took on the organistion of her own workshop in her own classroom.

The time spent on preparing materials for this interesting and rewarding form of collaboration must have been considerable. Obviously, much of the material can be used many times over so that in the second year of running a project of this sort less time is needed. Perhaps parents could be involved in making materials. The amount of worksheet material needed will depend partly on the reading approach adopted. The games and activities seemed in this case to be based on a phonic and a look and say approach to reading, and although the children did read to their mothers at the beginning of the workshop a good deal of the time was taken up with the more mechanical aspects of reading.

PARENTS AS WRITERS

Another, more unusual, way of involving parents in children's reading is evident in the project described in the article 'Parental Involvement in the Development of Language' (Clover and Gilbert, 1981). Parents wrote stories for their own children, were subsequently 'published' and shared in school.

The project began in Thomas Buxton School in Spitalfields in London in 1979. Being an inner city school, many of the children had mother tongues other than English. The school wanted to acknowledge and use this linguistic richness and also to involve its parents, bringing home and school closer.

Heather Sutton, working from the Thomas Coram Research Unit, had involved parents in writing books for their children in their home languages. The intention was now to build on this project and to encourage class teachers to collaborate with parents in this way.

Two class teachers in the school approached some of their parents about writing stories for their children and promised their help and support. They suggested that stories might be based on the child, the family, or on parent's memories of childhood.

It was most often mothers who volunteered and they would discuss the writing of the first draft with the teacher. Of course the project was not confined to those parents whose mother tongue was other than English. At this stage some mothers would come into the classroom and try out their first draft with a small group of children. Parent and teacher would edit the writing, and illustrations would be added. Sometimes another member of the family contributed towards this part of the book. The book would then be written into final draft or it might be typed. The book would then be covered and include a photograph of the child it was written for and also an autobiographical note on the author.

If the book was written in a language other than English, then a second copy would be produced in an English translation. Conversely, many books originally written in English would also be translated into other languages. In some instances the book was reproduced, giving more than one copy. If this was done the child would retain a copy at home. There would be a copy for the classroom and other copies for the school library and perhaps even for wider distribution into teachers' centres or the local community.

Several benefits seemed to be gained from this kind of project, which is surely an idea that many schools could take up. The production of books recognised and prized the cultural differences between groups of children, both in their languages and in their ways of life. Each child directly involved received a tremendous boost to their self-esteem and considerable motivation towards reading. As the children were part of the discussion and writing at home in the various stages, they had nearly always read the book by the time it was completed. Parent and teacher had worked together for the benefit of the child, and home and school had been brought closer together. Often the mother could be persuaded to read the book to the whole class and answer children's questions. The books had a freshness and immediacy which give them considerable appeal.

The ideas used in this project are now being tried out in the London Borough of Lambeth, where a group of heads and teachers from six schools, both infant and junior, collaborating.

It will be interesting to hear of reactions and further developments in this kind of work.

SUMMARY AND CONCLUSIONS

This chapter has looked briefly at some of the work that is taking place involving parents in children's reading in school. We have looked at a typical scheme for parents sharing reading in the classroom and two schemes which are more unusual. All these ways of working bring considerable benefits to the children involved and to the parents and teachers who collaborate.

When teachers invite parents into the classroom they are starting to break down barriers between home and school and also to 'demystify' the process and practice of reading. Preparation and organisation require much time and energy and we must be fairly sure that the benefits are commensurate with this. Many, many schools and teachers invite parents into school to be involved with children's reading. For every project that is written about, there are many instances of teachers working without fuss or recognition. It is a tribute to their professionalism that they take on this extended role.

SECTION IV

9 Preparation for partnership with parents

The check-list that is offered in Figure 9.1 is a reminder of the physical preparations necessary when initiating a home-reading scheme; it is also a source of pointers for discussion. As the case study in Chapter 3 showed, there may be considerable mental and even emotional preparation to be made before a successful scheme can be launched. The processes of thinking and discussion that lead on to the final, physical preparations are of enormous value in themselves, not only in developing ideas and approaches, but also in bringing the members of a school closer together.

PREPARING FOR COLLABORATION WITH PARENTS IN CHILDREN'S READING

Teachers and intending teachers when discussing collaboration with parents in children's reading, often display a hesitancy and diffidence about becoming involved in this kind of venture. For many teachers, working with parents is a new and, therefore, sometimes threatening part of their work. Whether or not teachers are going to collaborate with parents on children's reading, it is evident that there is a strong movement in education wishing to bring home and school closer and to encourage the voice of parents to be heard on the subject of their child's education. This movement was traced in Chapter 1 and there is no evidence of it weakening. It seems logical, therefore, that systematic attempts need to be made to help and encourage teachers to work with parents.

THE STUDENT TEACHER

There seems to be a patchy and uneven picture of systematic planning and implementation of courses that prepare intending teachers for work with parents. Many institutions of higher education are offering separate courses, or including in their general approach experiences that would help their students in this extended role. The main problem would seem to be what kind of experiences and teaching are (a) feasible, and (b) valuable. Many of these learning activities are of a generalised nature; they should be combined with a sound grasp of current thinking in reading and of projects showing collaboration between parents and teachers.

In their booklet *Preparing Teachers to Work with Parents*, Janet Atkin and

Figure 9.1 A check-list for a home reading scheme

Items of consideration	Consultation/ Discussion	Contacting sources of information/materials	Delegation of tasks	Preparations completed with date	Target date
PREPARATION					
1 *Materials*					
(a) Extra books:		Catalogues	Mrs —		Half term
(i) Which kind?		Visit Reading Centre	Everyone		Spring term
(ii) Financed by?		LEA adviser	Head		
		PTA	Head		
(b) Storage units for:					
(i) Books					
(ii) Correspondence					
(iii) Children's wallets					
(c) Guidance booklet for parents:		Univ. of Reading	Mrs —		
(i) Published		ILEA	Mrs —		
(ii) Made at school					
(d) Comment sheet for parents					
(e) Logo for scheme					

Items for consideration	Consultation/ Discussion	Contacting sources of information/materials	Delegation of tasks	Preparations completed with date	Target date
2 Explaining to children					
In class					
In assembly					
By displays and posters					
3 Contacting parents			Caretaker will make		
(a) Publicity board					
(b) First letter					
(c) First meetings:					
(i) Size of group					
(ii) Visiting speaker?					
(iii) Location					
(iv) Nature of					
(v) Timing					
(vi) Refreshments					
(vii) Materials, books and aids needed					
(viii) Translator					
CONTINUATION					
Frequency					
Writing in comment sheets					
Following up parents who do not attend meeting					
Home-visiting?					
Follow-up meetings (see first meetings)					

Holidays?
Lost books
Consultation times for
parents

EVALUATION

1 How?
   (a) Pre & post testing
   (b) Attitude tests
   (c) Using comment sheets
   (d) Teacher's log books
   (e) Feedback from parents
   (f) Feedback from children
   (g) Researcher?

2 When?

3 Why?
   (a) For school
   (b) For parents
   (c) For LEA
   (d) For continuation next
        year
   (e) For expansion of scheme

4 What?
   (a) Measured performance
   (b) Attitude change
   (c) Number of books being read
   (d) Discrimination in
        choosing
   (e) Better contacts with
        parents
   (f) More parental
        understanding

John Bastiani identify three models which operate in institutions for initial teacher education:

1 The permeation mode – where considerations of home-school relations, looking mainly at attitudes, permeate various courses.

2 Specific provision – where additional self-contained courses are offered.

3 The informal model – where approaches and coverage vary greatly between groups within institutions.

From their survey of 96 institutions, they found that one third of primary and one half of secondary students received no preparation for working with parents.

There are counter arguments which state that any kind of preparation for working with parents is inappropriate for the intending teacher because of age and inexperience. On the other hand, it would seem that by the fourth year of a BEd degree, or on a PGCE course, the intending teacher should be sufficiently mature to take on some work in this area. Like every other aspect of initial preparation for teaching, the matter cannot be left there, but needs to be revised and developed through in-service work.

It would seem sensible to conclude that this kind of learning could not take place with maximum effectiveness entirely within an institution. Immediately, then, there are factors of time and organisation to be taken into account and careful consideration should also be given to the delicate task of including students in consultations between parents and teachers.

For convenience sake, let us look briefly at the different kinds of learning activities that could be organised for the student teacher, firstly *in* and secondly *out of college*.

In college

1 Case study material can be used and discussed.

2 Video recordings of parents and teachers in various situations can be discussed. Extracts from the video from the ILEA about the Hackney PACT scheme might be useful here.

3 Glimpses of particular situations can be given to groups of students, who then reflect on and discuss their likely responses.

4 Activities 2 and 3 can be extended to develop into role play for students to gain more insight into parents' point of view. The kind of discussion situation that can lead to role play might be as follows:

Situation for discussion – 1

Background: A home-reading scheme is operating in your infant school.

Situation: One of the regular parents' evenings.

Person involved: Father of one of the children in your class.
Father: 'I think it's the teacher's job to teach children to read – not mine. That's what you get paid for, after all.'
Discussion: How would you respond?

Situation for discussion – 2

Background: The school is interested in asking parents to help with reading in the classroom.
Situation: A staff curriculum meeting.
Person involved: A colleague.
Colleague: 'I think it's chipping away at our professionalism – getting parents to come in and help us with reading. I've had years of training and experience . . . reading is my responsibility. Anyway I don't like other people in my classroom.'
Discussion: How would you respond?

Situation for discussion – 3

Background: Your school (infant or junior) runs a home-reading scheme. The children in your class usually choose their own books to take home.
Situation: After school one day.
Person involved: Mother of one of the children in your class.
Mother: 'The books that Jane is bringing home are too easy for her; can you give her something harder, please? She reads some of the books several times . . .'
Discussion: How would you respond?

Out of college

1   The college may be working along the lines of the IT/INSET (Initial Training/In-Service Education and Training) schemes, whereby groups of students work with their tutor and a teacher in the classroom, responding to school-based needs. This way of working is promoted by the Centre for Evaluation and Development in Teacher Education at Leicester University. The Director there is Dr Pat Ashton. This scheme would have the framework to introduce students and work with them and the teacher exploring collaboration with parents.

    Arrangements are made between some schools and colleges in partnership for small groups of students to join parents and teachers on occasions when parents come into school. Students could also accompany teachers on home visits. Time needs to be given to brief students before hand and to discuss the interaction afterwards. Of course, parents have to be consulted and their consent obtained in advance.

2   Some colleges make arrangements for individual or small groups of students to go into schools and classes where parents are involved with

children's reading. There they can join in the sessions and discuss the collaboration with parents and teachers. Here, again, the student has to be well prepared in advance.

3 A few colleges, in a real effort to show students that as teachers they need to appreciate children in their whole context, arrange, as part of a child study programme, for students to stay with a child in the child's own home for a short time. Students' perceptions of the child's whole life and relationships are inevitably deepened and sharpened as a result of this experience. This is a good base from which to explore the important relationship between teachers and parents.

Ideally, intending teachers should have opportunity for and help in preparing themselves for working with parents, both within college and 'in the field'. At the very least, however, students should not complete their initial preparation for teaching without developing an appreciation of the educative and supportive role of parents. They need to appreciate this role, particularly in the child's language development before and throughout the child's time at school.

Students approaching the completion of their initial preparation for teaching expressed these points of view:

1 they can certainly appreciate the value of collaborating with parents over children's reading. The students seem to be evenly divided as to whether they would be willing to start this immediately, or whether they would need time first to establish themselves with their class and within their school;

2 they would seem to be more likely to start collaborating with parents through a home-reading scheme rather than through working with parents in the classroom;

3 if they have not had the opportunity to look at working with parents in any systematic way, they certainly regret this omission as they come to start their teaching career.

THE PROBATIONARY TEACHER

Many heads now, when interviewing prospective new teachers, are concerned to know their candidates' views about involving parents in children's reading and about their willingness to do so. Where a school has, or is considering, a policy of collaboration with parents, it will certainly be hoping to appoint someone who shows some knowledge of and interest in this aspect of the teacher's role.

Many new teachers do invite parents into the classroom to help with reading. Most often this happens when it is the policy of the school to do so and where the presence and co-operation of parents is taken for granted. Here the new teacher is encouraged by the smooth co-operation she observes going on between colleagues and parents. She may also be actively helped and encouraged by a particular colleague who will advise and befriend her in the first year.

New teachers in infant schools who invite parents to help children in their early experiences of reading and writing arc clearly impressed with the contribution that parents can make. Most of these new teachers confess to being nervous initially, but say they soon gain confidence and start to appreciate the benefits of having more than one adult to whom children can relate.

MORE EXPERIENCED TEACHERS

Some teachers, for various reasons, do not become interested in collaborating with parents until they have had more experience in teaching. The most powerful source of help and information for them is probably another school or other teachers who are running successful schemes. Contact can be made informally or through the LEA advisers. Wider help and information can be obtained through sessions at local teachers' centres or local colleges. There is also a good deal of written material. Mention was made earlier in the book of teachers modelling their work on the reports of successful projects, such as those carried out in Haringey and Belfield. As a result of the Hackney PACT scheme there is both written material and a video that can be studied and discussed. Mention should also be made again of the CAPER project.

It does seem sometimes that individual, isolated schools or teachers who are doing good work could benefit tremendously from being in touch with others who are working with parents. Professional organisations such as UKRA, NATE and NAPE can be useful for making contacts and exchanging ideas, as well as informing their members of current research. Within the local authority, though, responsibility for this liaison often falls to the advisers, even though they are very hard-pressed. At the least, what is needed from the LEA is appreciation and continuing interest in teachers and schools taking on this work.

An alternative arrangement is for a head or teacher to take up a short-term fellowship at a local institution of higher education. There they could receive help and use time collating information from the schools in their area which involve parents in children's reading. From this work could come the organisation of joint meetings and the sharing of ideas and material. Indeed, in some areas this kind of work has already begun.

10 Conclusions

There is a thread that weaves through the fabric of this book – through the case studies, reports, discussions and suggestions. The underlying message is that *all* parents have a vital part to play in their child's education. This role is a continuation and a development of that of educator before the child begins formal schooling. The way in which this role develops is the responsibility of schools and individual teachers. It is up to schools to try to maintain the momentum of the partnership for as long as possible. Secondary schools are now endeavouring to continue this effort, particularly with chidren who are still experiencing reading difficulties.

There are moves now to involve parents in other areas of learning, particularly in maths, science and in writing, and it will be interesting to see how this evolves. There seems to be two main reasons why the focus has so far been on reading:

1 reading is seen by parents, children and teachers to have priority over all other learning that takes place in school;
2 reading is something that the vast majority of parents feel capable of helping with. After all, they have been readers for many years and reading is very much a part of their everyday lives.

This book has aimed to inform in several ways; most of all it has aimed to give a wide perspective on current developments in parent partnership and to present a realistic picture of what such a partnership might entail. Some well-known projects have been described as well as some more 'everyday' case studies. Both of these serve to give us inspiration, insight and points for discussion.

Every teacher knows that you cannot just take on board a package for partnership devised and worked through by other teachers and schools in other situations with their particular group of parents. In each situation the process of discussion, reflection, planning, setting aims and deciding on evaluation is different. The framework is the same but each situation needs its particular refinements.

The processes are valuable in their own right: as a way of being more understanding and effective; as a way of bringing the whole school together in one common purpose; and as a reason for opening up the whole question of reading. Partnerships that involve just one or two teachers and their parents do work but in a way that is obviously more limited. A pilot scheme that is begun in this way, though, may well be valid.

Parents and teachers have worked together in children's reading in different ways both based on the home and based on the school. They have worked together on behalf of children whose progress towards accomplished reading is smooth and also on behalf of children whose reading experiences have not been so happy.

The complexity of the partnership deepens, though, when parents work with teachers in school where many other factors have to be considered. Not least of these is a need to rethink the proposition that the primary school class should necessarily always consist of thirty children who turn to one adult only for their learning and language needs.

Student teachers need some preparation for working in partnership with parents and there seem to be some interesting and diverse methods in operation. Most students and tutors would feel that a start needs to be made in initial teacher education with further opportunities for development being offered both in their first school and through INSET.

The title of this book is *Partnership with Parents in Reading*; the word 'partnership' can be defined in more than one way. The actual nature of partnerships with parents in reading must also vary according to context. In the Concise Oxford Dictionary a partner is defined first as a 'sharer in something or with somebody'. In the case of parents and teachers they certainly share in the development of children's reading. In business terms 'partner' is defined as 'a sharer of risks and profits' – here, too, one can see the analogy with children's reading. 'Sleeping partner' implies 'the predominance of one partner over the other'. This is surely not the kind of partnership to be aimed at. The term 'senior partner' would ascribe more knowledge and experience to the teacher, perhaps, but the parent has more knowledge and experience of the individual child. A 'sharer' in children's reading seems to be the most satisfactory definition, with each partner bringing to the concern their own particular skills and attributes.

We have looked at what has now become a strong movement for parent-teacher partnership in children's reading. This exciting development in education provides potential for the extension of the role of the teacher and enrichment for the child's reading. Paradoxically, as the teacher recognises and accommodates the role of parents as educators, she extends her own role into new dimensions – if she will take the risk!

In one considered move, from 'allowing books home' to seeing parents as partners in children's reading, the teacher can set in motion a process which will benefit children far beyond an improvement in their reading skills. Beginning from an holistic view of reading, and recognising parents as educators, the teacher can *orchestrate* benefits for children's reading and promote closer links between home and school. The location for this partnership can be either in the home or in the classroom. When parents and teachers can work together in children's learning, there is no knowing where this partnership will end.

Appendix

‘FOOD’ HOME-LEARNING PACK
The following material, reproduced by kind permission of the South East
Coventry Community Education Project, was used as part of the home-
reading/learning scheme described in Chapter 5.

A HOME SCHOOL LEARNING PROJECT

FOOD

A HOME SCHOOL LEARNING PROGRAMME

Note for parents

The home school learning programme is not meant to be the usual idea of homework. It has been
worked out to help actual teaching points being used in your child's work this week.

Some points to remember

This booklet contains homework for one week. Only one page should be done each evening. Children
who complete the booklet may ask their teacher for extra sheets if they like doing the work.

The work is meant to be enjoyable for you both. Please do not force your child to do it.

Each page has a particular skill we are trying to help your child with.

Help your child as much as you can. Talk to him about each page. Help him towards the answers.
Tell him eventually if you have to. Help him to succeed.

Let us know the pages you both liked the best or the ones that were too hard. A reply sheet has
been included.

Help us to help your child.

SKILLS

These are some of the skills which your child will practice while doing these sheets.

Family Likes.

      Finding out information. Recording information. Following written
Family Dislikes.   instructions.

Plan a menu   Using the information discovered for a practical purpose.
Finding a compromise - balancing out peoples likes or dislikes,
instead of cooking a number of different meals.

Making Tea   Observation. Putting events in order without missing out any stages.
Representing information in picture form and writing instructions.

Clues   Working things out from clues and discussion with adults.
Realising that there may be more than one answer.

Where does it come from   Observation - looking at the tins etc., using an atlas to find out
where different towns and countries are.

Family Favourites

**Write your name on the first plate and make
a list of your favourite foods on the lines
above it.
Ask the rest of your family what their favourite
foods are. Write their names on a plate and
their choices on the lines above**

Family Dislikes

Write your name on the first plate and make a list of the foods you don't like on the lines above it. Ask the rest of your family which foods they dislike, put each name on a plate and write the foods above.

Use what you have found out about your family's likes and dislikes to plan an evening meal for each day of the week.

MENU

Monday

Tuesday

Wednesday

Thursday

Friday

Saturday

Sunday

Making a cup of tea

There are lots of different ways of making tea.

Watch one of your parents make a cup of tea.

Show how they do it by drawing in the cartoon strip.

Be careful not to miss out anything they do.

For example: Fetch the milk.

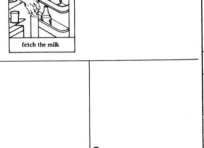

fetch the milk

1	**2**	**3**

6	
9	

10	**11**	**12**
13	**14**	**15**

Clues.

Here are some things bought from the shops each week by one family.

14 tins of baby breakfasts
 3 tins of dog food
 2 bottles of coke cola
 1 copy of a slimming magazine

What do these things tell you about this family? Remember sometimes you have to say 'I don't know'. Or ' I can't be sure '. There is often more than one possible answer.

Are there any children in the family?
Can you guess at about how old they are?
Can you work out what the family pet is?
Can you guess if it is big or small?
Do you know which child the pet belongs to?
Do you know if the family has any other pets?

Ask about the things your family buys each week. Write down the things that give clues to who is in your family – babies, children, teenagers, grown ups, old people, pets.

Make a list to show what you have found out.

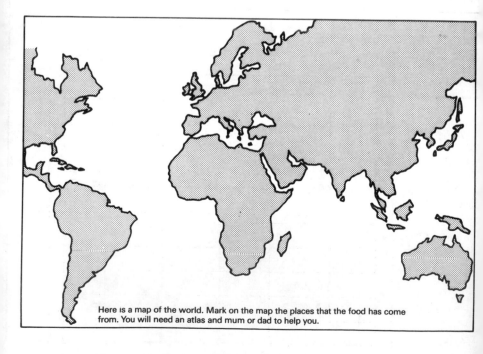

Here is a map of the world. Mark on the map the places that the food has come from. You will need an atlas and mum or dad to help you.

WHERE FROM?

The food in your kitchen at home comes from all over the world.

Have a close look at the labels on some tins (tins of fruit are especially good for this).

Ask your mum to keep labels for you.

Find out where the food came from, record it, and then mark the place on the map.

		which country?

Now try something else. Find out where some of your clothes came from.

article of clothing	where did you buy it?	which country?

Thank you very much for your help with this project.
We were delighted to know you spent so much time working together
with your child. Many of the children's enthusiasm carried over
into the classroom. A special thanks to those parents who commented
on the sheets. We have tried to take into account your suggestions
in producing this pack and we hope you will continue to let us know
your views.

DID YOU ENJOY IT?

General
Comments

Family Likes	Family Dislikes	Plan a Menu	Making Tea	Clues	Where does it come from

References and Bibliography

AHLBERG, J. and AHLBERG, A. (1977) *Burglar Bill*. London: Heinemann.
ATKIN, J. and BASTIANI, J. (1985) *Preparing Teachers to Work with Parents*. Nottingham University: School of Education, Nottingham.
BRANSTON, P. and PROVIS, M. (1986) *Children and Parents Enjoying Reading*. Sevenoaks: Hodder and Stoughton.
BUSHELL, R., MILLER, A. and ROBSON, D. (1982) 'Parents as remedial teachers', *Association of Educational Psychologists' Journal*, 5, 9: 7–13.
BUSHELL, R. *et al.* (1985) in TOPPING, K. and WOLFENDALE, S. (eds.) *Parental Involvement in Children's Reading*. Beckenham: Croom Helm.
CARLE, E. (1970) *The Very Hungry Caterpillar*. London: Hamish Hamilton.
CLARK, M. (1976) *Young Fluent Readers*. London: Heinemann Educational Books.
CLOVER, J. and GILBERT, S. (1981) 'Parental Involvement in the Development of Language', *Multiethnic Education Review*, Vol. 3, Winter/Spring. London: Inner London Education Authority.
DES (1967) *Children and their Primary Schools* (The Plowden Report). London: HMSO.
DES (1975) *A Language for Life* (The Bullock Report). London: HMSO.
DES (1977) *A New Partnership for our Schools* (The Taylor Report). London: HMSO.
DES (1984) *Parental Influences* (Green Paper) (Cmnd 9494). London: HMSO.
DOUGLAS, J. P. (1964) *The Home and the School*. London: MacGibbon and Kee Ltd.
DOUGLAS, J. P. (1968) *All our Future*. London: MacGibbon and Kee Ltd.
FREEMAN, J. (1976) *In and Out of Schools*. London: Methuen.
GARDNER, K. (1982) *Testing Reading Ability*. Nottingham University: School of Education, Nottingham.
GIPPS, C. and WOOD, R. (1981) 'The Testing of Reading in LEAs', *Educational Studies*, Vol. 7, No. 2.
GOODMAN, K. (1982) *Language and Literacy, Vol. 1*. London: Routledge and Kegan Paul.
GRIFFITHS, A. and HAMILTON, D. (1984) *Parent, Teacher, Child: Working Together in Children's Learning*. London: Methuen.
HEWISON, J. and TIZARD, S. (1980) 'Parental Involvement and Reading Attainment', *British Journal of Educational Psychology*, 50, pp. 209–15.
HUTCHINS, P. (1968) *Rosie's Walk*. London: The Bodley Head.
ILEA CENTRE FOR LANGUAGE IN PRIMARY EDUCATION (1984) *Read, Read, Read*. London: Inner London Education Authority.

ILEA PITFIELD PROJECT (1984) *Home-School Reading Partnerships in Hackney*. London: Inner London Education Authority.

INGHAM, J. (1981) *Books and Reading Development*. London: Heinemann Educational Books.

JACKSON, A. and HANNON, P. W. (1981) *The Belfield Reading Project*. Rochdale: Belfield Community Council.

MACKAY, D. *et al.* (1970) *Breakthrough to Literacy*. Harlow: Longman Group Ltd.

MEEK, M. (1982) *Learning to Read*. London: The Bodley Head.

MEEK, M. (1985) 'Play and Paradoxes, some considerations of imagination and language', in WELLS, G. and NICHOLLS, J. (eds.) *Language and Learning*. Lewes: Falmer Press Ltd.

MIDWINTER, E. (1977) *Education for Sale*. London: Allen and Unwin.

MOON, C. (1977) *Individualised Reading*. University of Reading: Centre for Teaching of Reading.

NEALE, M. D. (1958) *Analysis of Reading Ability*. Windsor: NFER/Nelson.

NEWSON, J. and NEWSON, E. (1977) *Perspectives on School at Seven Years Old*. London: Allen and Unwin.

NUT (1983) *Home/School Relations and Adults in Schools*. London: National Union of Teachers.

ORMEROD, J. (ed.) (1983) *Moonlight* and *Sunshine*. London: Penguin.

SALLIS, J. (1978) *Parents and School*. London: BBC Publications.

SCHOFIELD, W. (1979) *Haringey Reading Project*. Final report to DES.

SMITH, F. (1978) *Reading*. Cambridge: Cambridge University Press.

SOUTHGATE, V. *et al.* (1981) *Extending Beginning Reading*. London: Heinemann.

STIERER, B. (1985) 'School Reading Volunteers', *Journal of Research in Reading* (UKRA), Vol. 8, No. 1, February.

STIERER, B. (1985) 'Parental Help with Reading in Schools Project'. Unpublished report to Education and Human Development Committee of the Social Science Research Council.

TIZARD, B. and HUGHES, M. (1984) *Young Children Learning*. London: Fontana.

TOPPING, K. and WOLFENDALE, S. (eds.) (1985) *Parental Involvement in Children's Reading*. Beckenham: Croom Helm.

WATERLAND, L. (1985) *Read With Me*. Stroud: The Thimble Press.

WEINBERGER, J. (1983) *Foxhill Reading Workshop*. London: Family Service Units.

WELLS, G. (1982) *Language, Learning and Education*. University of Bristol: Department of Education, Bristol.

WELLS, G. and NICHOLLS, J. (eds.) (1985) *Language and Learning*. Lewes: Falmer Press Ltd.

WHILBY, P. (1981) 'The Belfield Experiment', *The Sunday Times*, 26 March.

WIDLAKE, P. and MACLEOD, F. (1984) *Raising Standards*. Coventry: Community Education Development Centre.

YOUNG, D. (1969) *Group Reading Test*. Sevenoaks: Hodder and Stoughton.

Index